Effective Reading

Reading skills for advanced students

Teacher's Book

Simon Greenall and Michael Swan

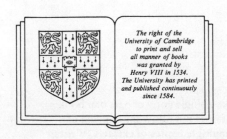

The right of the
University of Cambridge
to print and sell
all manner of books
was granted by
Henry VIII in 1534.
The University has printed
and published continuously
since 1584.

Cambridge University Press
Cambridge
London   New York   New Rochelle
Melbourne   Sydney

Published by the Press Syndicate of the University of Cambridge
The Pitt Building, Trumpington Street, Cambridge CB2 1RP
32 East 57th Street, New York, NY 10022, USA
10 Stamford Road, Oakleigh, Melbourne 3166, Australia

© Cambridge University Press 1986

First published 1986

Printed in Great Britain at the Bath Press, Avon

ISBN 0 521 31760 6 Teacher's Book
ISBN 0 521 31759 2 Student's Book

WD

Contents

Contents

Introduction

This book is intended for teachers using *Effective Reading* either as
supplementary skills material or as the basis of an advanced level English
course. It contains:
– a description of the problems involved in reading a foreign language,
  and an explanation of the techniques and exercise types which are used
  in this book to help students read more effectively.
– a unit-by-unit guide, including ideas on how to make the most of the
  material, background notes (where necessary) on the passages, and an
  answer key.

Reading effectively

Everyone reads with some kind of purpose in mind: for instance, to keep
up with the news, to obtain specific information, or simply for pleasure.
A reader's purpose may also include the need to reproduce the content of
the text in some way or other: in a discussion of the ideas it contains, for
example; or in summarising the text for a report or an examination.
Effective reading means being able to read accurately and efficiently,
understanding as much of a text as one needs in order to achieve one's
purpose. Not everybody can do this even in his or her own language. In a
foreign language, the problems are of course greater, and comprehension
failure is common. This may be a simple matter of not knowing a word,
but it is equally likely to be due to a deficiency in one or more of a number
of specific reading techniques. The exercises in this book are grouped
under headings which refer to these specific techniques.

Extracting main ideas

Sometimes it is difficult for a student to see what the main ideas of a
passage are, or to distinguish between important and unimportant information. The exercises in this section encourage students to read for the
general sense rather than for the meaning of every word.

Reading for specific information

It is not always necessary to read the whole of a text, especially if one is looking for information which is needed for a specific purpose. The activities under this heading set the student a variety of different tasks in order to practise this type of reading.

Understanding text organisation

A student may sometimes have trouble in seeing how a passage is organised. These exercises give practice in recognising how sentences are joined together to make paragraphs, how paragraphs are combined into text, and how this organisation is signalled.

Predicting

Before reading a text we usually subconsciously ask ourselves what we know about the subject matter. This makes it easier to see what information is new to us and what we already know, as we read the passage. If we can help students, where necessary, to transfer this skill to a foreign language, we can ensure that as they read they are not overloaded with too much new information.

Checking comprehension

Under certain circumstances (such as in examinations) a student may need to study a passage very closely in order to answer a question correctly, and exact understanding of points of detail may be crucial. The exercises in this section train students in this kind of careful reading.

Inferring

A writer may decide to suggest something indirectly rather than state it directly. The reader is required to infer this information – which may be essential for correct understanding. Some students may need practice in seeing such implications.

Dealing with unfamiliar words

One of the commonest problems facing a student is simply not being able to understand a word or expression. But it is often possible to guess its general sense by looking for clues, either in the context or in the form of the word itself. Exercises in this section develop the techniques needed to make reasoned guesses about the meaning of new vocabulary.

Linking ideas

In any passage an idea may be expressed by a number of different words or expressions. The exercises here give the student practice in seeing how different words are related to the same idea.

Understanding complex sentences

Some writers, consciously or unconsciously, use a complicated style in which it may be difficult, for example, to distinguish main clauses from subordinate clauses. Struggling with complex syntax can make it easy to lose sight of the general sense of the text. In this section, the student is given practice in 'decoding' long and complicated sentences.

Understanding writer's style

An important part of the pleasure in reading is being able to appreciate why a writer chooses a certain word or expression and how he/she uses it. A number of stylistic devices and features are discussed in this section.

Evaluating the text

A full understanding of a passage may depend on appreciating why it was written, or what purpose particular parts of the text serve. It may, for instance, be important to distinguish between a statement of fact and an expression of the writer's opinion. This section helps develop the student's more critical faculties.

Reacting to the text

Sometimes a reader's interpretation of a passage may be coloured by his or her own views on the subject being dealt with. In this section, practice is given in separating what the writer says from what the reader thinks.

Writing summaries

The ability to write an accurate summary requires accurate comprehension of a passage, the ability to distinguish between essential and secondary information, and skill in composing clear, economical text. For students who need this technique (which is required, for instance, for the Cambridge Certificate of Proficiency examination) special training is provided.

How to use *Effective Reading* in class

It is important to remember two points. Firstly, not every student has the same reading difficulties, and not everyone will want or need to do every section and exercise in a unit. We hope that the book contains sufficiently varied material to allow the students to choose what techniques they need to practise. It will usually be more practical for you to select the passage to be studied, but if possible, encourage the students to do only the sections which appeal to them most. If you see that a student is regularly doing well in the exercises of a particular section, it may be that he/she has already acquired this specific reading technique, and doesn't need to practise it any more. So suggest that the student tries a different section next time. Secondly, the aim of this book is to *teach* rather than to *test* reading ability. So the process by which students arrive at their answers is often more important than the answers themselves. For this reason, passages which students find easy are just as useful to them as passages which they find more difficult.

The units have been grouped in threes according to their general theme; the themes are shown in the *Summary of units and techniques* and in the *Contents* of the Student's Book. Students may not find it interesting to do every unit in a group, so you may decide to move on to another theme in order to maintain their motivation.

The passages are also *loosely* graded according to their lexical or structural difficulty. For example, students in the year leading up to the Cambridge Certificate of Proficiency examination may find the units in the first half of the book a little easy. However, there is also a progression in the difficulty of the exercise types in the different sections. So it would be better for everyone to do at least units 1–6, where there are some important techniques explained. We hope that even if the passage itself presents little difficulty, the exercise types will be useful and motivating.

If you allow your students to do different sections in a unit, there will be a problem in organising your correction of their work in class. To resolve this difficulty at least partially, ask your students to work with people who are likely to need practice in the same techniques. They can compare notes, discuss their answers and thus do some self-correction. Try not to demand the attention of the whole class to correct exercises that have only been done by some of the students; visit the groups as much as possible and correct their work individually.

In the unit-by-unit guide there are some suggestions on how to present and exploit the passages for other skills work, and to integrate the passages into an advanced course. If you were to do every section in a unit, excluding the suggestions for *Further work*, it would take between 60 and 90 minutes. However, a more balanced lesson using material from

Effective Reading would include the following:
– Some kind of warm-up/discussion activity to introduce the topic.
– Work on a selection of the techniques covered by the unit, which will
  generate vocabulary development, guided and free writing activities, as
  well as some oral practice, since most of the exercises are performed in
  pairs or small groups.
– A follow-up activity taken from the *Further work* section, such as a
  group discussion, a roleplay or project work.
In addition to this, some extra listening practice or grammar revision
may be necessary.

Summary of units and techniques

	Extracting main ideas	Reading for specific information	Understanding text organisation	Predicting	Checking comprehension	Inferring	Dealing with unfamiliar words	Linking ideas	Understanding complex sentences	Understanding writer's style	Evaluating the text	Reacting to the text	Writing summaries	
People and personalities														
1 Doodles	x	x					x						x	1
2 Money is the only home	x		x				x			x				2
3 Shielding Brooke	x		x			x	x							3
Food and drink														
4 The good picnic guide	x					x				x			x	4
5 Down and Out in Paris and London			x			x	x	x						5
6 A family lunch in Beirut	x	x	x				x							6
Houses and safety at home														
7 House for sale	x	x	x		x									7
8 Burgled seven times			x	x	x				x				x	8
9 Sissinghurst Castle	x		x	x			x		x					9
Jobs and employment														
10 24 hours in the life of the City		x	x			x		x			x			10
11 How to write a winning résumé	x						x	x					x*	11
12 All Greek to me	x							x			x		x	12
Shopping, consumer affairs, advertising														
13 Shopping basket psychology	x		x	x				x					x	13
14 Mr Hornby's casebook			x			x	x				x	x	x	14
15 Commercial break	xxx					xx					x			15
Travel														
16 This way for suite dreams	x			x			x			x				16
17 Clearing customs		x				x						x	x	17
18 Getting China cracked	x	x					x						x	18
Wildlife and the environment														
19 The capybara	x					x	x	x		x			x	19
20 Save the jungle – save the world	x			x		x	x	x		x				20

	21	22	23	24	25	26	27	28	29	30	31	32	33	34	35	36	37	38	39	40	41	42	43	44	45
21 Beware the dirty seas																									
Medicine and physical condition																									
22 The sword that can heal																									
23 How to live to be a hundred																									
24 How to help the hard of hearing																									
Transport																									
25 Sorry sir, sorry, sorry																									
26 Go steady on the gas!																									
27 The Trans-Siberian Express																									
The arts and leisure activities																									
28 On show																									
29 Indiana Jones and the Temple of Doom																									
30 An away win																									
The media																									
31 Should the Press be human?																									
32 Pregnant Di still wants divorce!																									
33 How do you feel?																									
Formal and informal education																									
34 Childhood: pathways of discovery																									
35 Village voice																									
36 Boys are teachers' pets																									
Taste, fashion and design																									
37 Good taste, bad taste																									
38 Shot at dawn																									
39 Absolute musts																									
Legal systems, law enforcement, crime																									
40 Trials and errors																									
41 Arresting scenes in Bombay																									
42 Streetwise																									
Racism, ageism, right or wrong																									
43 When a sense of nationhood...																									
44 Lucy Rowan's mother																									
45 Looking on the bright side																									

Unit 1   Doodles

Before you begin this unit, you may like to introduce the topic.
Draw the following shapes on the board:

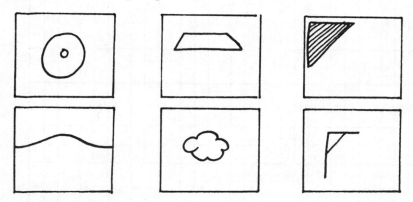

Then ask the students to copy *one* or *two* of the drawings. Explain that
the drawings are 'unfinished' and need to be 'finished' in whatever way
the students find most appealing.

This warm-up will give you the basis for a discussion on the students'
own doodles. It's important to do this activity *before* you begin the unit
in the book, in order to make sure that the students' doodles are as
unconscious as possible.

Extracting main ideas

This section will encourage your students to read for the general sense of
each paragraph, which is 'summarised' in the form of a picture. The
technique of extracting main ideas is the first stage in writing summaries.
Try to avoid answering any specific vocabulary questions for the
moment.

Answers:
3 1H 2E 3F 4A 5G 6D 7I 8B 9C

Reading for specific information

You may like to explain that we don't always read something from beginning to end; sometimes we read selectively, looking for the answer to a specific question.

Possible answers:
a) affectionate: paragraph H   c) disorganised: paragraph J
b) cruel: paragraph C   d) happy: paragraph E

If the students have done the warm-up activity, ask them to work in pairs and decide what the passage says about each other's doodles. They should also discuss whether the character analysis is accurate or not.

Dealing with unfamiliar words

Explain to your students that this section has two purposes:
i)   to help them understand selected words in the passage;
ii) to present two useful techniques for dealing with unfamiliar words.
You may also want to mention that it is better not to rely on using the dictionary all the time; in this section, it should only be used in the last part of exercise 3.

Answers

	angular	inherent	ailment	gregariousness	embellishments	repressing	muddlehead
1	adj.	adj.	noun	noun	noun	verb	noun
2	i	ii	iii	ii	ii	i	i

Some of the answers are not exact synonyms of the words in the questions. You may need to explain that it isn't always necessary to understand the exact meaning of a word or expression.

Writing summaries

This section practises a similar skill to that found in *Extracting main ideas*; some students may have to develop their techniques of reading a passage for its general sense into an ability to write summaries, particularly for examinations such as the Cambridge Proficiency exam.   ⫸→

Answers to 1 and 2:

webs	feel trapped −, lack confidence −
circular formations	eternal love +, faithfulness +, idealism +, need to reproduce +
knives, daggers, guns	aggressive behaviour −, sadistic −, masochistic −
trees and landscapes	lack of warmth −, spiritual weariness, ill −, disappointed in love −
faces	sociability +, outgoing +, sentimental + , grumpy −, anti-social −, gregariousness +, shyness ±, reserve ±
houses	seeking emotional security −, lacking in love −, houseproud +, untidy −, secure +, happy +
filled in or shaded doodles	aggression −, anger −, sarcasm −, defensive −
hearts, flowers, animals	in love +, daydreaming +, sentimental +, kind +, affectionate +, spontaneous +
heavily lined shapes	barrier between you and the world −, emotions under control +
confused lines and squiggles	muddlehead −, can't cope −, lack of self-control −

After completing 3, and if you have done the warm-up activity, you can ask your students to write a short paragraph describing their partner's doodle.

Further work

It may be better to do this activity for homework. If possible, encourage the students to do the preparation in groups of two or three. Before you leave this topic, find out whether they think this kind of character analysis can be useful or not.

Unit 2   Money is the only home

This passage is taken from a novel by Stephen Vizinczey called *An Innocent Millionaire*, which is the story of a young man's search for some treasure buried under the sea. During his search, he gets to know a very rich young woman called Marianne Hardwick.

Extracting main ideas

Encourage the students to discuss their answers to this question. You may find that they do not agree on the correct answer, but the exercise will nevertheless generate some meaningful discussion.

Suggested answer:
c)   The rich still have families because of the influence of their money (but some people may choose (e)).

Dealing with unfamiliar words

In unit 1 we looked at two techniques for dealing with unfamiliar words. The exercises in this section give further practice in these techniques. Remember that it is the techniques which are important here rather than the actual explanation of difficult words or expressions. Encourage your students to work in pairs as much as possible and to help each other work out the meaning of any other difficult vocabulary without using a dictionary.

Answers:
3 a) vi   b) viii   c) ii   d) iii   e) vii

Understanding text organisation

It is sometimes difficult to see how longer sentences are organised because subordinate clauses may conceal the main clauses. On other occasions it may be difficult to see how two parts of a passage or a sentence are joined together because the link words are implied rather than stated directly.

1 Read the sentences aloud to the students without pausing at the commas; ask them to note down the main verb in each sentence without
  looking at their books. You can remind them how commas usually
  indicate a pause in spoken language, and that the pauses are used to
  make the sentence easier to understand by indicating sense groups.

  Answers:
  a) are   b) is

2 'Though they have . . . ' (lines 15–18)
  They may have the boldest manners and most up-to-date ideas, *but*
  they share their grandmothers' humble dependence.

3 *Because* girls were not meant to fend for themselves, he protected them
  from life.

4 'Prevented from acquiring . . . ' (lines 11–15)
  Because they are prevented from acquiring the habits of freedom . . .
  very rich girls . . . are the last representatives of Victorian womanhood.

Encourage them to do the exercise in this section in pairs.

Understanding writer's style

Some students may find it difficult to appreciate the use of irony in this
text. What is happening here is that the author is quoting, often without
comment, words and expressions used by (or attributed to) rich people
like Creighton Montgomery, which reveal their character and attitudes.
The words therefore have a double meaning: that given them by the rich,
and the very different significance that they have for the writer and the
reader.

Answers:
a) The writer does not feel that girls were not meant to fend for them-
    selves; this is the view of Creighton Montgomery and people like him.
b) The writer feels that this is a strange kind of 'protection' – he calls it
    'crippling'.
c) The writer is implying that the rich regard themselves as rather like
    gods (who are not mortal).
d) The writer does not think that the 'sound views' of the tutors who
    support Victorian values are sound at all.

Further work

You may like to organise a discussion on the role of the family in everyday life. If you have students from different countries in the group, make use of their views in order to build up a broad picture of family life all over the world.

Unit 3   Shielding Brooke

This passage is as much about 'star quality' as about the film actress, Brooke Shields. To introduce the topic, bring to the class a number of magazine photographs of famous people: actors, musicians, entertainers. Ask your students to form groups of two or three. Hold up each photograph in turn and ask them to discuss why they think each person is famous and whether they deserve their fame.

Understanding text organisation

This exercise type is designed to help students become more aware of how the passage is organised. The missing sentences can only logically fill in one blank space. It is a good idea to let students do this exercise alone first of all, and then for them to check their answers with another student.

Answers:
1 1d   2f   3a   4h   5e   6g   7b   8c

Extracting main ideas

This exercise is to help students practise reading for the general sense; the titles are a kind of summary of each paragraph. To prepare them for the exercise, you can ask them to note down three or four key words in each paragraph which express its most important ideas. Then ask them to check their answers with another student.

Answers:
paragraph 1: e   paragraph 2: c   paragraph 3: g   paragraph 4: h
paragraph 5: a   paragraph 6: i   paragraph 7: b   paragraph 8: f
paragraph 9: d

Dealing with unfamiliar words

This section's aim is to show you don't always need to know what every word or expression means in order to understand the general sense of a passage or a sentence. This point is made clearer if the distracting words are removed.

Possible answers:
1 Clearly the point of the exercise is that there can be a number of different answers; here are some suggestions:

   b) stare, look, gaze   e) clever, intelligent, brainy
   c) woman, actress, siren   f) -self, childhood, shell
   d) has, possesses, inherited

It's a good idea to let the students discuss the alternative answers as much as possible. Some answers may not be acceptable for a variety of different reasons, and this may need to be explained.

Inferring

You may need to explain to your students that information is sometimes implied rather than stated directly. This is a bit like 'reading between the lines', and some students may find this exercise type a little difficult to begin with. But implied meaning can be an important source of information in a passage, and students will have plenty of other opportunities to practise this skill elsewhere in the book.

Answers:
b) The writer says that Brooke's mother is ' . . . cheerfully large, big-breasted, plump' (lines 19–20), and that 'Brooke's (. . .) looks come from her father's side' (sentence h), and therefore not from her mother.
c) Brooke's mother was 'managing a small restaurant' (lines 44–5) when she met Frank Shields; she is now managing Brooke and 'since 1980, their average income has been $1 million.' (lines 50–2)
d) Frank and Teri's marriage 'only lasted a few weeks after Brooke was born' (sentence (e)) and Frank has now remarried; so Teri and Frank no longer live together.
e) The passage says ' . . . will Brookie (. . .) come out of her shell . . . ' (lines 68–70) which suggests that she is still quite shy even though she is eighteen years old.
f) We learn that Teri 'stage-manages' interviews (lines 15–16) and that she has 'built up her daughter's career . . . ' (lines 23–4)

Further work

The writing activity in 3 is a way of letting the students choose what vocabulary items they want to learn; this should help them to learn more effectively than if you were simply to give them a list of useful words. It is also a way of organising their vocabulary notes; the three passages in units 1, 2 and 3 all deal with people and personalities, and one way of organising their vocabulary learning would be to group the new items under this heading. As your students go through the three passages noting down the new vocabulary, keep a record of some of the words and expressions which they choose. This will be useful for revision and testing purposes later, or to help you predict which words and expressions are likely to cause problems in future units.

Unit 4   The good picnic guide

The passage was written by Keith Waterhouse, who is a journalist,
novelist and playwright. It comes from a book called *Mondays,
Thursdays*, which is a collection of some of the articles he has written for
the *Daily Mirror*.

Before you begin reading this passage, it may be necessary just to check
that everyone knows what a picnic is. If there are one or two people who
don't know, tell the others to look through the passage and choose two
or three words or expressions which give an idea of what a picnic might
be: for example, 'meal' (line 10) 'countryside' (line 85). Make sure you
don't spend too long on this activity; 30 seconds scanning the passage is
probably sufficient. Then write these words or expressions on the board,
and see if all the students now understand what a picnic is. Even if
everyone knows what a picnic is, this is quite a useful warm-up activity.

Extracting main ideas

You may want to remind your students that the point of exercises in the
Extracting main ideas sections is to encourage them to read for general
sense. So try not to answer any questions on specific vocabulary items.
The passage may be a little difficult, but you can tell them that they do not
have to understand every word.

Encourage them to discuss the answer to this question in pairs.

Answer:
d) A meal eaten outdoors on a sunny day in the country surrounded by
    children who are allowed to do whatever they wish.

Inferring

You may need to point out that some of the statements in this question
are false in reference to the passage. The exercise is to practise inferring
information but also to discourage careless readers from inferring information which isn't in the passage. If they find this activity difficult, give a

17

time limit of about five minutes to the exercise and then discuss the
answers with the whole of the class.

Answers:
b)   No evidence; the writer suggests that the Japanese are able to eat at
     tables without legs without getting indigestion.
c)   True; the writer says that 'Children are (. . .) useful for fetching
     cigarettes' (lines 28–30)
d)   True; the writer mentions that picnics should have a 'proper air of
     adventure' (lines 42–3) and then goes on to describe how the children
     should be allowed to behave.
e)   True; the food that the writer describes in lines 53–67 is more attract-
     ive and tasty than nutritious. He also says that it will be 'lacking in
     vitamins.' (line 109)
f)   True; the writer says there should be 'streams to fall in, trees to fall
     out of . . . ' (lines 39–43)
g)   True; the writer says 'A picnic is not sandwiches.' (line 15)
h)   True; in describing what the writer thinks is the best kind of picnic, he
     writes 'You will feel bloated and dyspeptic for your picnic will have
     been stodgy and messy . . . ' (lines 107–9)

Understanding writer's style

The writer intends to be humorous in this passage, but this aspect may be
overlooked by your students if they are more interested in answering the
various questions. If you think they are taking the passage too seriously,
it may be better to move straight to 2 and discuss whether they find this
passage amusing, and if so, why. If they don't find the passage amusing
or interesting, it may be a suitable occasion to discuss what makes people
laugh, and whether they enjoy English and American humour.

Answers:
1   a) i   b) i   c) ii   d) ii   e) i
2   Some examples: 'Anyway, you've forgotten the mayonnaise.' (lines
                   13–14)
                   '. . . as well as coming in useful for fetching cigarettes.'
                   (lines 29–30)
                   ' . . . provided that they are not boringly whole-
                   some . . . ' (lines 62–3)
                   ' . . . who has been crazed with hunger ever since . . . '
                   (lines 70–2)

Writing summaries

This exercise is designed to show that some kind of structure is needed for summary writing. In this case, a lot of the important information is given in the form of accurate statements about the passage. The students can then build on this structure by reading the passage again to see if anything has been left out.

Answers:
1 a) true   b) false   c) true   d) false   e) true   f) true   g) false
   h) false   i) false   j) true   k) true   l) true   m) false
2 Order of accurate statements: f c a j e l k

Further work

This activity is particularly enjoyable if you are organising a picnic that actually takes place!

Unit 5   Down and Out in Paris and London

You might introduce the passage by explaining that George Orwell is most famous for his novels *Animal Farm* and *Nineteen Eighty-Four*. Ask students if they have heard of or read either of these novels. Orwell regarded his own background as relatively privileged, so he decided to find out what it was like living on very little money; *Down and Out in Paris and London* is an account of his experiences. The passage begins after he had been living in Paris for some time, but before he found work doing the washing up in a large hotel.

As a warm-up, you can ask people to write down what they would buy if they only had £1 to live on each day. (Tell them their accommodation is free, but not their food.)

Understanding text organisation

Your students may find this exercise type a little difficult to begin with, and you may want to help them by saying *where* the intruding sentences should go. In the exercise, the intruding sentences simply don't make logical sense where they are to be found; by deciding which are the intruding sentences and where they should go, the students are encouraged to recognise the logical organisation of the passage.

Answers:
b) 'There is nothing for it but to throw the milk away and go foodless.' (lines 13–14) should go after ' . . . straight into the milk.' (lines 5–6)
c) 'Bread is a franc a pound, and you have exactly a franc.' (line 16) should go after ' . . . paying two sous extra?' (line 11)
d) 'For half a day at a time you lie on your bed feeling like the *jeune squelette* in Baudelaire's poem' (lines 21–2) should go after ' . . . can interest yourself in nothing.' (lines 37–8)
e) 'With bread and margarine in your belly you go out and look into shop windows' (lines 25–6) should go after ' . . . to be hungry.' (line 28)
f) 'It is hours before you dare venture into a baker's shop again.' (lines 6–7) should go after ' . . . you bolt in panic.' (line 13)

Inferring

Answers:
a) No evidence; there is no suggestion that the writer lied about his poverty, but he did choose to conceal it from others.
b) True; the spirit lamp (lines 3–4) suggests that there is no oven or properly equipped kitchen.
c) No evidence; he was unlikely to deliberately spoil the milk he was boiling.
d) True; otherwise he wouldn't have thrown the milk away (see lines 13–14).
e) True; he left the baker's in a hurry when he realised that he might have to pay more than he could afford for the bread.
f) True; see line 8.
g) No evidence; the baker's girl is merely described as being clumsy by cutting more than a pound of bread.
h) True; although the writer only describes one example of what might happen in a baker's shop, it is clearly one of a number of 'mean disasters' which are part of the process of being hard up.
i) True; the word 'slink' (line 18) suggests that he left the shop in embarrassment.
j) No evidence; it is more likely that he was embarrassed to be seen by them.
k) True; see lines 38–41.
l) No evidence; he didn't take the bread because he was scared of getting caught.
m) No evidence; if you have no money, according to the writer, you have nothing to do and the only thing which really interests you is food.
n) No evidence; the writer only suggests that a lot of people live in the suburbs of poverty.

Dealing with unfamiliar words

The purpose of this section is to present and practise a technique rather than explain the meaning of all the difficult words in the passage. Remind the students, if necessary, of how the context can be used to guess the general sense of an unfamiliar word or expression.

Answers:
1 a) enter   b) leave   c) leave   d) enter   e) enter
2 a) i   b) i   c) ii   d) iii   e) ii

Linking ideas

This exercise is designed to give students practice in deciding what pronouns refer to. Ask your students to do the exercise on their own and then to check their answers with another student.

Answers:

a) The bug.
b) One franc two sous.
c) Pay the extra.
d) Those which occur when you don't have very much money.
e) Life on six francs a day.
f) Life on six francs a day.

Further work

These activities will give the students plenty of practice in the oral skills. Try and introduce as much cross-cultural information as possible. It may be necessary to tell the students to use reference books to find out relevant information. It doesn't matter if the research for a project like this is done with books in your students' native language(s).

Unit 6   A family lunch in Beirut

It may be necessary to check that everyone in your class knows where Beirut is and that there has been a civil war in the country for some time. This passage was written in 1982. To introduce the topic, ask your students what they think everyday life must be like in a town or a country which is at war. Ask them to imagine what their own towns would be like if the situation in Beirut was happening there.

Understanding text organisation

This exercise type is similar to the one in unit 3, but here there are no blanks to indicate where the missing sentences should go. Ask your students to do the exercise on their own to begin with, and then to check their answers with another student.

Answers:
Sentence a should go after ' . . . prohibitively expensive.' (lines 55–6)
Sentence b should go after ' . . . normal life and family customs.' (lines 23–4)
Sentence c should go before 'Mme Saidi makes quick forays out of the kitchen . . . ' (lines 68–9)
Sentence d should go after ' . . . as if by conjuror's trick.' (lines 84–5)
Sentence e should go after ' . . . for one kilo.' (lines 66–7)
Sentence f should go after ' . . . for the customary Friday lunch.' (lines 6–7)
Sentence g should go after ' . . . everyone is together.' (lines 73–4)
Sentence h should go after ' . . . half a dozen variations of 'mjederah.' (lines 49–50)

Extracting main ideas

In this exercise the most suitable title is an accurate summary of the passage itself. If students suggest more than one title, ask them to justify their choice.

Answer:
Celebrating survival over the dinner table.

Dealing with unfamiliar words

The exercises in this section are designed to demonstrate a technique –
looking for clues to the meaning of unfamiliar words in the context –
rather than to provide an explanation of every new vocabulary item. In 1
it may not be necessary to find a suitable word to explain the words and
expressions in the left hand column. Encourage the students to discuss the
likely meaning and if necessary to paraphrase it, saying 'It means something like . . . ' or 'It has something to do with . . . '

Reading for specific information

You may want to explain that we don't always read a passage from
beginning to end; sometimes we scan it looking for specific information
to answer a question.

Answers:
1 Lentils, aubergines, courgettes, ground wheat, onions.
  You can ask your students what the main ingredients in their country's
  cooking are.

2 a) kibbinayeh b) lbnimu
  This is an activity to check the students' understanding of what is
  meant by the various ingredients, rather than their knowledge of
  Lebanese cooking.

Further work

The passages in units 4, 5 and 6 have all dealt with one aspect of food and
drink. You may like to point this out to your students so that they can
organise their vocabulary lists. As they look through these passages, go
round and note down some of the words which they have learnt. You
may want to include these items in a vocabulary test or revision activity.

Unit 7   House for sale

As an introduction to this unit, you can ask your students to draw the ground plan of the house or flat where they live. Then tell them to describe this ground plan to another student without showing it.

Checking comprehension

1 This activity is designed to check the students' comprehension of the house descriptions by matching them to the suitable illustration. They will have to look closely at the descriptions because some of the houses differ only in one or two details.

Answers:
1 B   2 A   3 F   4 D

When you have finished this exercise, you might like to ask them if they are likely to find these kinds of houses in their own countries.

2 This exercise should be done alone. Go round the class checking that everyone has understood both the vocabulary in the descriptions and the aim of this exercise.

3 This part of the exercise should only take about five minutes.

Extracting main ideas

Answers:
1 A1   B5   C12   D3   E7   F8   G4   H2   I10   J9   K6   L11

The main point of this article is to describe which points will add value to a property, and which points will not. It's very important to discuss with the students whether the points mentioned would be relevant to houses and flats in their own countries. ⟫→

Improvements which add value	*Improvements which don't add value*
gas-fired central heating	electric/oil-fired central heating
first garage	double glazing
bathroom/inside toilet in an extension to the house	garden improvements
	second/third garage
increased accommodation and living area attached to the house	kitchen improvements
	nuclear air raid shelter
	bathroom/toilet which replaces an existing bedroom
	thermal insulation / heating improvements
	solar heating
	replacement windows
	swimming pool

Reading for specific information

As the instructions suggest, the students are meant to look for information in the passage which concerns the house they chose in 2 of *Checking comprehension*. However, it may be that some students might like to read the passage for specific information concerning aspects of their own home.

It's possible that the features mentioned in this passage have little relation to anything in the students' own country or countries. It might be a good idea to discuss how you might change the passage so that it refers to typical homes in their countries.

Understanding text organisation

You may like to explain that the words in capital letters in these two exercises signal the organisation of a sentence.

Answers:
1 a) Everyone wants central heating as long as it is a gas-fired system.
   b) Oil-fired central heating might be acceptable to buyers if it can be converted to gas.
   c) You can increase accommodation and living area cheaply provided you use the existing walls of the house.
   d) Bathroom and toilet improvements are attractive as long as they are in an extension to the house.

2 a) Solar heating is not particularly attractive to buyers but it might
      warm the water in the swimming pool.
   b) Electric central heating is economical in new houses although it is
      bad news in a thirty-year-old house.
   c) Cutting noise nuisance is double glazing's real value although it
      will be years before the initial cash outlay is recouped.
   d) It is true that garden improvements are very attractive but they
      don't put much on the resale value.

Further work

The aim of these activities is to allow students oral practice in discussing
the broader aspects of buying and selling property. Encourage them to
talk as much as possible about their own countries, rather than insisting
they talk about Britain and America.

Unit 8 Burgled seven times

To introduce the topic of this unit, ask students if they have ever been burgled or know of anyone who has. Ask them for their views on the social causes of burglary and the psychological consequences on the householder.

Predicting

You may like to explain to your students that if they write down ten or fifteen words which they expect to see, or think of things which will prevent burglary, they will prepare themselves better for the reading task and understand more about the passage.

Encourage students to do this section in groups of two or three and to compare their answers to 1 and 2 with other groups.

Understanding text organisation

This exercise may look difficult at first, but the students will soon realise that the sequencing nouns and adjectives *first*, *second*, *third* etc. will help them. Ask them to do this exercise in pairs.

Answers:
Sentence a should go after ' . . . and to the railway line.' (lines 21–2)
Sentence b should go after ' . . . which he suggested.' (lines 27–8)
Sentence c should go after ' . . . and a cassette player.' (line 34)
Sentence d should go after ' . . . but not in the flat.' (line 57)
Sentence e should go after ' . . . around the local streets.' (line 99)

Ask them to justify their answers. What clues did they find in the context?

Checking comprehension

This exercise makes sure that the students have read the passage carefully. Ask them to check their answers with another student when they have finished.

Answers:
a) True; this is suggested by the fact that Fel is well known in the local glass merchants, because she's always buying new panes of glass to mend her broken windows. (lines 1–2)
b) We don't know; the passage says only 'one of the other 21 flats in her *block* has been burlged' (lines 9–11) although later it says that a 'magistrate living near Clapham Common . . . has been burgled 18 times in two years.' (lines 85–8)
c) True; 'only one of the other 21 flats in her block has been burgled; and the previous occupant of her flat lived there for 40 years without being burgled once' (lines 9–14). Also, the police said 'it wasn't natural to suffer like this.' (lines 80–1)
d) False; 'the place is everything the burglars love.' (lines 15–16)
e) We don't know; all we know is that the neighbour called her while she was at her mother's. (lines 35–7)
f) We don't know; the passage only says that Fel's MP blamed unemployment. (line 50)
g) True; the police connected an alarm 'at their own expense.' (line 54)
h) True; the passage says she 'slept very lightly' (lines 95–6) presumably because she was scared of being burgled at night.
i) False; the passage says 'the alarm went off as the burglars tried the sitting room' and we assume that they were frightened off. Note also 'That *would have* been a real clean-up job.' (lines 100–1)

Understanding complex sentences

This section looks at the difficulties that sentences with subordinate clauses and lists (such as the features of Fel's flat in (a)) can cause. The commas very often represent a pause in spoken English; consequently, the students are advised to read the sentences aloud. If they work in pairs, Student A should choose sentences a and b, and decide where the commas should go. He/she should then read it aloud to Student B, who should mark the commas according to the pauses. Student B should do the same with sentences c and d.

Writing summaries

Encourage students to read the passage for its general sense and to think of questions they might ask a householder about his/her property when giving advice on how to beat the burglar.   ⟫→

Possible questions:
Do you live in a house or flat? Is there ground floor access to your
    property?
Do you have locks on every door and window?
Do you have many valuable items?
What kinds of precautions do you take when you go away on holiday?
Do you know your neighbours well enough to ask them to keep an eye on
    your home when you're away?

Further work

You may like to give students some time during homework to prepare
their views on the causes of burglary. Get them to discuss their opinions
in a class debate.

Unit 9   Sissinghurst Castle

Most people visit Sissinghurst Castle because of its beautiful garden, which the passage describes. To introduce the topic, you may like to ask if any of your students like gardening, or if there are any famous gardens in their countries which are open to the public.

Extracting main ideas

This exercise requires the student to select a suitable title with the help of the map after reading each paragraph for its general sense. Understanding the general sense is particularly important in this unit, because the language is likely to cause many students some difficulty; there are even words such as 'pleached limes' which some native speakers would not understand exactly.

Answers:
A e   B f   C g   D h   E k   F d   G i   H a   I b   J j   K l   L c

Understanding text organisation ·

This exercise gives practice in using visual information (the map) to work out how a passage is organised.

Answers:
G H K A I B F E J D L C

Dealing with unfamiliar words

It may be worth mentioning to your students that deciding what family a word belongs to is a similar technique to guessing its general sense. ⟫→

Answers:

plants/types of trees	oak, lime, box, rose, azaleas, shrubs, yew, herbs, aromatic plants, magnolias
architectural features	staircase, tower, turrets, room, entrance, courtyard, garden, path, cottage, wing, arch, gateway, window, fireplace, chimney, door, wall

Understanding complex sentences

This section looks at some of the difficulties that long sentences with several subordinate clauses can cause. As in unit 2 *Understanding text organisation*, the pauses in spoken English which organise the sentence into sense groups are represented by commas in written English. You may like to point out that good punctuation is particularly important if you are writing more complicated sentences.

Answers:
2 a) Before August 1573.   b) All these features.   c) A pathway.
   d) Either left or right.

Further work

The passages in units 7, 8 and 9 have dealt with different aspects of houses and safety at home. Your students may like to organise their vocabulary notes under this heading. As we have seen in all these units, it is necessary to use the English setting of the passages as a stimulus for a discussion about the students' own country or countries. The passages are meant to be interesting, but they are not necessarily meant to present a culturally biased view of the world! Do involve your students' own experiences and opinions as much as possible.

Unit 10   24 hours in the life of the City

Before you begin this unit, you may like to point out that the City of London is the oldest district in London. If possible, show them where the City is on the map. You can also explain that there is also another city in London, known as the City of Westminster; the other districts are known as boroughs. If your students know quite a bit about London, test their general knowledge by asking them to decide whether the following places are in the City of London, or the City of Westminster.

Tower Bridge (City)   The Houses of Parliament (Westminster)
Trafalgar Square   St Paul's Cathedral (City)
  (Westminster)   Big Ben (Westminster)
London Bridge (City)

Now write up seven or eight times of the day on the board, e.g. 8 a.m., 10.30 a.m., 1 p.m., 3 p.m., 6 p.m., 7.30 p.m., 9 p.m., 11.30 p.m. Ask students in turn to describe what they would be doing at these times during a normal working day.

Reading for specific information

If you haven't yet been able to use a map to show where the City of London is, you may like to explain that the one shown in the Student's Book shows the limits of the City of London. Westminster and the West End lie outside the map to the left, and Tower Bridge is in the bottom right hand corner.

Answers:
1 c) Barbican Arts Centre (this is part of a large residential complex and includes two theatres, a number of cinemas, an exhibition and conference area.)
2 d) Snow Hill police station.
3 f) Post Office.
4 b) St Paul's underground station (your students may remember St Paul's Cathedral as the large domed church in the centre of the City).
5 g) Sweetings fish restaurant.   ⋙→

33

6 a) Financial Times office (the *Financial Times* is a daily newspaper dealing mainly with financial and commercial matters, particularly Stock Exchange reports).
7 e) Lloyds (this is the most important insurance corporation in the world, dealing with marine and aviation insurance as well as some of the more exotic risks explained in the article).

Understanding text organisation

As your students do the exercise, ask them to note down any words which help them to put the sentences in the right position.

Answers:
Sentence a should go after ' . . . dramatically increased.' (lines 60–1)
Sentence b should go after ' . . . with people.' (line 4)
Sentence c should go after ' . . . during the day.' (lines 53–4)
Sentence d should go after 'A varied bunch.' (lines 87–8)

Linking ideas

You may want to explain to your students that it is sometimes difficult to decide what certain words or expressions refer to.

Answers:
a)   The fall in the Dow Jones index (which is the index showing the rise or fall in the value of shares on the American Stock Exchange in Wall Street, New York).
b)   To get to St Paul's underground station.
c)   The residents of the City of London.
d)   A varied bunch of risks to insure.
e)   The fact that the City's working day ends earlier than most of the rest of London; the working day.

Inferring

Answers:
a)   She joined the police force to work with people but on the night shift, there aren't any people around.
b)   The editor doesn't wish to create a false market, as people make big investment decisions on what they read in the *Financial Times*. This suggests that it takes care to give accurate reports.

c) John Milne has to come by bus in order to get to the underground station by 5.25 a.m., to open it.
d) 'Then it's on to the second delivery around midday.' (lines 54–5)
e) The passage says the 'tiny number of residents.' (lines 57–8)
f) The passage refers to the strains of the harp and flute being an 'overture to the night's activities.' (lines 103–5)

Evaluating the text

This section will help students to appreciate matters of style and the intention of the passage.

Answers:
1 i   2 c

Further work

Your students may have found the passage interesting not only for its description of life in the City of London, but also for the useful vocabulary. Spend as much time as you think is necessary on the first suggestion in this section. You may like to use the passage as the basis of a project to describe a day in the working life of the town you are in at the moment, which will encourage the students to work in groups, possibly going out and interviewing people doing typical jobs. If you have a large class, divide them into groups of three or four, and ask them to prepare their project, then to report to the rest of the class, and to discuss the different groups' conclusions.

Unit 11 How to write a winning résumé

The advice on writing résumés in this passage may be particularly relevant to your students if they are still at school or don't have a job at the moment. Even if they are working, you can always discuss whether you think the advice given is good or not, or suitable for job-hunting in your students' countries. You may want to point out that a résumé is called a c.v. (curriculum vitae) in Britain.

Extracting main ideas

The slang expressions in this passage may cause particular difficulties, so it is important to help your students read for the general sense and not to concentrate too much on literal meaning.

Answers:
Paragraph a goes under the heading 'Turn bad news into good.' (line 49)
Paragraph b goes under the heading 'Be specific, be concrete, and be
    brief.' (lines 47–8)
Paragraph c goes under the heading 'Sell what you can do, not who you
    are.' (lines 30–1)
Paragraph d goes under the heading 'Put yourself first.' (line 26)

Before you go on to the next section, see whether your students can give a brief résumé of what each heading means. You may like to ask them to take down the key words in each of the paragraphs to practise their summary skills.

Dealing with unfamiliar words

As we have seen in the section above, the literal meaning of some of these expressions may be a little obscure. Explain that many native speakers would only fully understand these expressions once they had seen them in the context.

Answers:
a) ii b) iii c) i d) i e) iii f) ii

Linking ideas

Answers:
a) Two kinds of résumé.
b) Everyone has abilities.
c) Abilities.
d) What you have written about yourself.
e) A printed résumé.

Writing summaries

This exercise has been included in order to give the students something to write about in a 'simulated' résumé. Of course, it would be more interesting for the students to make similar notes about their own career, objectives and skills etc., even if they have no real need to write a résumé. Alternatively, you may like to take a few interesting job advertisements from newspapers and ask students to write a fictitious résumé for the post that interests them most of all. If there is more than one candidate for a particular post, ask the students to work in groups and to decide which candidate has written the best résumé.

If you decide to use the notes suggested in the Student's Book, students are likely to include the following:

Vocational objectives
Maybe a job as customer relations manager?
Could work as administrative assistant.

Money management skills
Co-ordinated fund raising in town.
Invested an inheritance for 20% annual return.
Look after family budget and save 10% of yearly income.
Raised money for local church.

Summary of background
Attended Indiana University.
Studied business administration at night school.
Specialised in business application of computers.
20 years raising two children.
Worked for 3 years as secretary to manager of sales division, ABC company.
promoted to administrative assistant.

Competitive and team skills
Sing in church choir.
Have run 5 marathons.
Like working in a team.

Management skills
Chairperson of son's school Parent-Teachers' Association.
Helped husband reorganise his filing system by installing micro-
    computer.

They will probably leave out: Left after one semester! Not sure what I'd
be good at doing! Hated secretarial work! Get bored quickly. Like flower
arranging. 42 years old and only 5 years salaried employment!!!

Further work

If this is useful, use the *Further work* discussion to share ideas on how to
get the job you want.

Unit 12   All Greek to me

You may need to explain that a tycoon is a very rich and powerful businessman, and that the Greek tycoon of the film title refers indirectly to Aristotle Onassis, the Greek shipowner who married Jacqueline Kennedy, the widow of the assassinated President of the United States of America. Ask your students if they can think of any tycoons in their own countries. What kinds of businesses do they run? If there aren't any tycoons, can they think of the reasons why?

   This passage is fairly difficult for students at lower levels, so you may find it useful to ask them to work separately, and then in small groups to discuss their answers, and finally as a class.

Extracting main ideas

You may like to point out that each one of these statements is in fact true, but only one, as the question says, is an accurate summary of the passage.

Answer:
d) There are a surprising number of people involved in making films, and a good example of this is *The Greek Tycoon*.

Linking ideas

Answers:
1 a)   The exact function of 'best boy'.
   b)   Credits; a good example of how some films can have few credits.
   c)   The fact that the film has eighty-three credits.
   d)   The number of people involved with the music.
   e)   Unit publicist and two assistants.
   f)   The fact that the film was made in three locations.
   g)   The film.

$\ggg\!\to$

2 a) Technical credits.
  b) Categories of technical credits.
  c) More people involved with the music.
  d) Disputes about who does which job.
  e) A lot of people who give orders and only a few people who carry
      them out.

Evaluating the text

1 Obviously, the writer's humorous intentions may not always be
  successful, so it may be useful to discuss whether the students find
  parts or all of the passage funny or not.
  The jobs which the author finds particularly strange are: 'gaffer'
  (line 9), 'best boy' (line 10), 'Controller' (line 23), the various types of
  producer (lines 26–31), the various types of musical directors (lines
  41–83), 'Location Production Runner' (lines 89–90), 'Producers'
  Driver' (lines 91–2).

2 The writer does not like the film at all. The expression 'That stank'
  (line 104) is slang meaning the film was extremely bad.

Writing summaries

This exercise type is to help students develop their summary skills without
actually having to write a summary. Choosing what information to
include is an important part of summary writing. As in the exercise in
Extracting main ideas, both summaries of each paragraph are adequate,
but one is slightly more accurate and concise than the other.

Answers:
a) i   b) ii   c) i   d) ii   e) i

Further work

As in the activities in units 10 and 11, which also deal with the theme of
jobs, some of the questions in this section may be difficult to do if some
or all of your students don't have jobs at the moment. If this is the case,
you may like to ask your students to interview suitable people who have
got jobs and to present their conclusions to the rest of the class. This
preparation can be carried out in their own languages as long as they
work in groups and report back to the class in English.

Unit 13 Shopping basket psychology

To introduce the topic, ask your students how often they go shopping, where they do their shopping and why. Then ask them to make a list of what they would buy in a typical week. This list can be kept for the activity in the *Further work* section of this unit.

Predicting

You may like to explain to your students that a great deal of information can be obtained by reading the title and thinking how much they know about the topic, by checking whether they know anything about the author, and by asking where the passage is likely to be found, what they think the purpose of the passage is (to inform, to entertain, to teach), whether they think the topic is likely to interest them) and similar questions in order to prepare them for the passage. If the students write down ten or fifteen words which they expect to see, these words will create a structure of ideas which will allow them to prepare themselves for what the writer is likely to say.

Similarly, if the students read the passage in short sections and then reflect on what the writer is likely to say next, they are more likely to understand better what he says, whether they predicted correctly or not.

Encourage the students to discuss the answers to these questions in groups of two or three.

Extracting main ideas

Before you ask your students to do this exercise, you can suggest that they write down five or six key ideas expressing the main point, if possible without looking back at the passage. Ask them to do this in groups. Then ask them to look at the sentences and see whether any of them contain a number of the key ideas they have written down.

Answer:
c) 'If body language can tell a stranger a lot about one's personality, so can the fruits of your shopping expedition.'

41

Understanding text organisation

This is quite a difficult exercise, but a useful one. The different uses of the adverbs refer to the function of the sentence and its relevance to the rest of the paragraph.

Answers:
a) type A   b) type B   c) type A   d) type B   e) type B   f) type A

Linking ideas

Answers:
'basket' (line 8), 'selections' (line 9), 'mixed bag' (line 16), 'fruits of your shopping expedition' (lines 43–4), 'choice' (line 80), 'cart' (line 89).

Writing summaries

It may be useful to explain that a summary can very often be organised in the way which is shown in the Student's Book, even if the passage itself is not. For summaries with a very strict word limit, it is advisable to leave out the *exposition* section.

Your students may answer the questions with the following notes:
a)   contents of writer's shopping basket generating hostility – fairly luxurious/expensive items; writer shocked at contents of woman's basket – convenience/ready prepared food
b)   a lot about your personality, life style, situation
c)   star-struck shopper, gourmet bachelor, young housewife, the person who only buys frozen food
d)   try and imagine the life style of the person in front

Now that your students are starting to write summaries on their own, you may like to suggest that they look at each other's finished versions. It is probably better if you don't hand round the summaries for everyone to see, as this may discourage the weaker students. But comments from a trusted partner may be a useful way of improving their summary skills.

Further work

You may have already asked the students to write their weekly shopping lists; use them to perform this activity. Do they think it is a more accurate way of analysing life styles and even personality than, for example, looking at doodles (unit 1)?

You can also discuss with your class the ways in which you might be able to make shopping more economical and efficient. Discuss ways of making shopping lists, going to the shops, deciding what to buy etc. What recommendations would you ask shop owners to make in order to make shopping a more pleasant or efficient task?

Unit 14   Mr Hornby's casebook

This is a fairly short passage but it may generate a lot of amusement and interest. If you have a particularly creative group, you may like to ask them to turn the story into a short sketch.

Before you begin, ask them if they have ever had any trouble in getting something mended, replaced or serviced in some way. Think about cars, clothes, electrical equipment, furniture or similar products. What is likely to go wrong with them? How easy is it to have the problem cleared up?

Inferring

Answers:

b) True; the antique shops in this area of London are willing to do repairs, but for themselves not for the public.

c) True; the fact that the man in the second shop was 'slightly politer' (line 25) suggests that the man in the first shop was rather rude.

d) No evidence; he decided that his approach or style was wrong.

e) True; he placed it carefully on the floor so as not to disturb the damaged leg.

f) True; this is implied by the way the man accepted the writer's price for the chair.

g) No evidence; the writer had entered the fifth shop with a plan, and the plan was to buy the chair back when it was repaired.

h) True; apparently, he didn't do repairs because there wasn't enough money in it.

Dealing with unfamiliar words

Most of the vocabulary in this passage is fairly straightforward. If your students think so too, ask them to choose four or five words and to think of synonyms for them; they then give the list of synonyms to another student who should find the words in the passage. (This is similar to the activity in unit 12.)

Answers:
a) i   b) iii   c) i   d) iii   e) ii   f) i   g) i   h) ii   i) i

Understanding text organisation

Answers:
a) Yes, I saw that *but* it's nothing.
b) I like the bit of old green velvet on the top *so* I shall leave that.
c) It is just what I'm looking for, *so* I'll give you 27 quid for it.
d) We don't do repairs *because* there's not enough money in it.

Writing summaries

This is an easier summary exercise to do than the one in unit 13, but it will help the students concentrate on the link words and the organisation of the sentences in relation to one another. To make this more lively, you may like to write out the sentences on separate cards and give one card to each student (or pair). They should then walk round saying their sentences aloud, trying to work out the correct order without looking at the sentences.

Suggested answers:
c) Mr Hornby had a chair with a broken leg *but*   g) he didn't expect any difficulty in getting it mended. *However*   f) to his surprise, none of the first four shops he tried were prepared to do the repair. *So*   b) in the fifth shop, he tried selling the chair rather than asking for it to be mended. *But*   e) when the proprietor agreed to buy it and had explained what he would do with it, Mr Hornby offered to buy it back. *Then*   a) the proprietor suddenly realised Mr Hornby wanted to have the chair mended rather than sell it. *So*   d) amused by the whole episode, he agreed to mend it for £5.

Evaluating the text

Answers:
1 Because it needed hard work and determination to get the chair mended.
2 a) obstinate, good-humoured, ingenious
   b) unhelpful
   c) good-humoured

Further work

You may like to suggest that in addition to or as an alternative to the
proposed activities, the students work in groups to prepare a short sketch
on another consumer service situation such as: getting a brand new
hairdryer changed because it doesn't work, complaining about a stain
that appears on a suit after it has been cleaned, changing a pair of shoes
that are almost new but which leak, questioning a large garage bill for a
simple job such as an oil change.

How many of your students also like to collect or keep antique
furniture? How many prefer to have modern furniture? Discuss the
advantages and disadvantages of both types of furniture.

Unit 15   Commercial break

A very simple warm-up for this unit would be to spread a number of
photographs taken from magazines around the class. Then ask the
students to work in pairs or groups of three and to choose two or three
photographs. They must then try and decide what the photograph might
be an advertisement for. You can finally ask them to write a few words
for the advertisement's slogan.

Ask the class to describe which advertising medium is the most
effective. Think about magazines, newspapers, television, radio, posters
etc. How many students can remember buying a product for the first time
only because of an effective advertising campaign?

Extracting main ideas

There is obviously no correct answer to this question but the original
advertisement used 'Irish or Scotch. Which is the more romantic?'
You may want to discuss whether the other slogans might be more
suitable.

Inferring

Answers
a) No; when the woman asks for a Jameson, the writer replies' "Oh," I
   said somewhat blankly', which suggests that he had never heard of the
   whiskey.
b) The woman and the Jameson whiskey.
c) The writer is probably not very young as he writes 'I felt about sixteen
   again . . . '
d) Not at first; he writes 'And before rejoining my partner I took a little
   sip – just to see if she was right', which suggests that he wasn't sure
   whether he would like Jameson's.
e) It could be both Jameson's whiskey and the woman.

You may like to end this section by asking your students whether they
think this advertisement is successful or not.

Extracting main ideas

Remind the students that all of these statements are true, but only one of them expresses the main idea of the whole advertisement.

Answer:
d) Crest Hotels take great care in looking after businesswomen as well as businessmen.

Before you continue with the next advertisement, you may like to discuss the kind of problems that businesswomen may have when they are on business trips. Have any of your female students travelled on business?

Inferring

Answers:
a) Usually they're put behind a pillar or near the kitchen door, which is regarded as being one of the worst places in a restaurant.
b) Usually they have to take their briefcases into the bar to show that they are in the hotel for business rather than social reasons.
c) The 'softer' decor suggests that other hotels are decorated in brighter colours.
d) Articles like hairdryers and irons are often too bulky to carry in your luggage.
e) Their attitude is described as 'businesslike'.

Once again, ask your students if they find this advertisement effective.

Extracting main ideas

You may need to explain that this advertisement is for the British Army and that, in Britain, the army is a professional one and relies on the same kind of recruitment procedures as any other employer. There is no compulsory military service.

Answer:
d) It appeals to the patriotism of the reader to join the army and defend his country and the free world.

You may like to ask your students whether they think this kind of advertisement is acceptable as well as being effective, or whether it uses a far too emotional appeal. Ask them if they think this kind of advertisement for the army or for the other armed forces could appear in a newspaper in their own countries.

Evaluating the text

After dealing with each advertisement, you may have asked the students whether they find it effective or not. This section is designed to make them reflect more precisely on the exact nature and intention of each of the three advertisements.

There are no right or wrong answers to this question.

Reacting to the text

This letter refers to the final advertisement in this unit, the one for the British Army.

Further work

You may find that you have already discussed the effects of advertising sufficiently. Either you can show a few more examples of advertisements taken from magazines and newspapers and ask the students to write a short paragraph discussing whether they are effective or not, or you can pass straight on to 2, which refers to the theme of units 13 and 14 as well as this one.

Unit 16   This way for suite dreams

You may like to explain that 'suite' in the title of this passage refers to a suite of rooms in a hotel, but is also a play on words with the expression 'sweet dreams', which is what you say to people when you hope they will have a good night's sleep.

Ask your students whether they have stayed in hotels very often, if at all. Which hotel was their favourite, and which one was the worst they have ever stayed in?

Predicting

As in unit 13, a lot of information about a passage can be obtained by looking at the title, thinking about the topic and predicting what is likely to appear in the passage. Some of these words or expressions are at first sight unlikely to appear in a passage about hotels, and the students may find it interesting to see how the writer manages to include them, often in a very amusing way.

Extracting main ideas

Answers:
1 paragraph A: dream
    paragraph B: nightmare
    paragraph C: dream
    paragraph D: dream
    paragraph E: nightmare
    paragraph F: nightmare
    paragraph G: nightmare

⟫→

2 (*Suggested answers:*)

	Dream hotel	Nightmare hotel
hotel service	Speed and willingness with which they do their job. Monastic silence.	Very slow. Man at desk doesn't know what room service is.
food	Hot.	Yesterday's scones, tepid tea.
lifts	Small, well-stocked bar. Music.	Operated by female hammer-throwers. 15-minute wait. Operator pretends not to see you and closes doors in your face.
restaurant service	Guest does not use hands.	Waitresses who lean against concrete columns and won't serve you.

Dealing with unfamiliar words

There may be a number of words which your students will not understand in this passage. Decide whether you want to make use of it as a means of increasing their vocabulary, or whether you want them to read it for its general sense. The words and expressions explained in this section are possibly the most important items which need to be understood.

Answers:
1 a) i   b) ii   c) i   d) ii
2 a) iii   b) vi   c) i   d) ii   e) iv   f) v

If you decide that you do want students to use the passage as a way of increasing their vocabulary, let them choose the words they want to learn. But it is nevertheless better if you limit the number of new words. This will not only limit the amount of time spent on the exercise, but also encourage them to work out the meaning of some of these words without looking them up in a dictionary.

Understanding writer's style

Some of your students may not necessarily find this passage amusing. Nevertheless, it is a good idea to encourage them to notice at least when the writer is *trying* to be funny!

Possible answers:
1 ' . . . this function is performed by an élite corps of deaf mutes . . . '
   (lines 8–10) – **praise**.
   'During the time it takes to come you can write a novel, go bald, change
   sex, perhaps even retire.' (lines 34–6) – **criticism**.
   ' . . . a certain type of South Korean geisha house . . . use his hands.'
   (lines 44–8) – **praise**.
   ' . . . the machines themselves seem to have borrowed various important design details from the people who invented the padded cell.'
   (lines 65–9) – **criticism**.
   Note that there are a number of other examples of humorous or
   exaggerated descriptions in this passage.

2 a) i   b) ii   c) i   d) ii

Further work

It doesn't matter if some of your students have never stayed in a hotel; the
questions are meant to encourage fictitious descriptions if necessary.

Unit 17 Clearing customs

This passage is about the experiences of people in foreign countries. You may like to introduce the topic by asking your students to describe briefly their experiences when they went to a foreign country for the first time. What did they find particularly strange about their visit? What did they think foreigners might find strange about their own countries?

Reading for specific information

This section is to encourage students to look for information in answer to a specific question rather than to read the passage from beginning to end. If they only spend about three minutes on this exercise, they can read it more carefully a second time and still leave themselves plenty of time to do the other exercises.

Reacting to the text

A passage like this will inevitably provoke a lot of discussion and maybe even some disagreement. This should be encouraged if you wish to provide some motivating oral practice.

If you have time, you may like to ask them to write down a few notes in answer to the questions and then to present their ideas in a more formal discussion with the rest of the class.

Inferring

You may want to remind the students that the questions refer only to what is said in the passage, and not to what the students may think the passage *ought* to say. After you have done this exercise, you may want to discuss whether there are any errors in the passage, and how they should be corrected. ⟫→

Answers:

a) No evidence; the passage says that you should not drink more than three cups of coffee.

b) True; according to the passage, visitors will sometimes come into the office in the middle of a meeting with someone else.

c) No evidence; the passage says that the British expect visitors to know when to leave without telling them.

d) True; according to the passage, offices are closed between 1 p.m. and 4 p.m.

e) True; you should leave without making too much fuss, according to the passage.

f) No evidence; the passage says that you will be invited to take a sauna if a good business relationship has been established. It doesn't say that you won't need a swimming costume on other occasions.

g) True; in certain countries, according to the passage, they mean you are in love with the person you are giving them to.

h) True; according to the passage, however, the wives expect to be invited even if they decline.

i) No evidence; however, the passage suggests that you should at least offer to pay.

j) True; according to the passage, it's even considered an insult to do so.

Writing summaries

The first part of this exercise is similar to an *Extracting main ideas* exercise type. You may want to remind your students that it is essential to note down the general sense of a passage before they begin writing their summaries.

Answers:

	business protocol	social customs	gifts	clothing/appearance	eating/drinking
Middle East	Other visitors will sometimes come into office during meeting. Visitor should try to pick up the check.*	The word 'no' must be mentioned 3 times.			Impolite to drink more than 3 cups of coffee unless your host drinks more.
Britain	Considered impolite to interrupt a visitor.				
Spain	You should offer samples of your goods. Offices closed 1–4.30 p.m.			You should wear black shoes and dark clothes.	
Indonesia	You should present business cards (in 2 languages).				
Japan	You should expect to distribute up to 40 cards a day.	Certain guests will leave early. Let them leave discreetly.			
France	You should list your academic credentials on business cards, Organise a 'special occasion' after a deal.		Send flowers but not chrysan-themums.		
Scandinavia		You may be invited to take a sauna. Gifts should be sent the following day (Norway).	In Denmark take flowers or a delicacy if you're invited.		
West Germany		Men stand when ladies leave the room.	Take flowers but NOT red roses.		
Switzerland			You can take roses but not 3.		
Korea		Wives are invited but expected to decline invitations.			Guests of honor* are served first. But the privilege must be declined once or twice.
Mexico					Keep hands on table.
China		Friendship is expressed by clapping.	It's an insult to give gifts.		
Singapore				Men with long hair and beards aren't welcome.	
Soviet Union					

*Note: 'check' and 'honor' are American spellings, British spellings are 'cheque' and 'honour'.

Further work

You may like to discuss some of the gestures which can mean different things in different countries.

Unit 18 Getting China cracked

To introduce the topic, you may like to ask your students what they know about China, and to gather as much information as possible by writing it on the board. Ask about population (approximately one billion people), capital city (Beijing), size of the country (third largest in the world after the USSR and Canada) and any facts that people might know about the politics, climate, education, the media, the Cultural Revolution, religion, trade and commerce, shopping, food, tourist sights etc. It is surprising how much information a 'brainstorming' session of this kind generates; remember also that it isn't essential for all the facts to be accurate. If there is any information which is not covered by the reading passage in this unit, you may like to ask students to find out more about the country for homework.

Extracting main ideas

Answers:
1 D 2 L 3 J 4 M 5 F 6 B 7 C 8 K 9 H 10 A 11 G 12 O
13 I 14 E 15 N

Reading for specific information

Although some students may find most, if not all of this passage interesting, people who actually intend to go to China are likely to read only parts of it. This exercise is designed to encourage students to find answers to specific questions as effectively and quickly as possible. The time limit is set in order to make sure that they are not distracted by inessential information.

Answers:
a) Hotels with dormitories which cost about 6 yuan per night. (see paragraph L)
b) Yes, it can be crisp and sunny in the North while it is balmy in Hong Kong. (see paragraph M) ⟫→

c) Yes, by bicycle, bus or by train, but you will need a permit. (see paragraph D)

d) Only the common cold which is stronger in Asia than in the West. There are herbal remedies or Western medicines (available in the large cities), but it's a good idea to take personal medicine and toilet articles with you. (see paragraph I)

e) If you go out on your own, you'll find the Chinese very hospitable. (see paragraph A)
Many young people speak English and will want to try out their conversation skills on English speaking visitors. (see paragraph J)

f) The food is more varied and better than the Chinese food usually found in the West. (see paragraph F)
Look for a place to sit down and then point to the dishes you want to try. (see paragraph B)

g) The yuan; there are about 3 yuan to the pound sterling. (see paragraph L)

Dealing with unfamiliar words

Words to complete these sentences can be easily guessed from the context; your students are likely to find that if they don't guess the exact word, they will guess a word that means more or less the same. Point out to them once again that it isn't always necessary to understand, or even to see all the words in the passage.

Answers:

a) hospitable, escorted
b) soppy, batty
c) puritanical, misdemeanours
d) unpromising
e) cluster
f) balmy

Writing summaries

Answers:

	recommended	not recommended
transport	Bicycles, buses, trains.	
sightseeing	Beijing, the Great Wall, even industrial cities.	
accommodation	Luxury hotels, Chinese hotels which accept foreign 'individual travellers'.	
weather/seasons	Good weather in October. Crisp and cold in winter in the north, warm in the south, unpredictable weather in the spring.	October is the busiest month for tourists.
food	In the north, Mongolian hot pot, or heavy meat dumplings. In Sichuan, special dishes.	Food served to foreigners in hotels.
restaurants	Major and ordinary. Eat at midday or between 5.30 and 7 p.m.	
entertainment	At operas, the costumes are glorious and audience-participation, total.	The operas are incomprehensible and uninteresting
shopping	Silk goods and jewellery. Try the Friendship stores.	
personal health and safety	Medical facilities are good in major cities. Take personal medicine with you.	Don't get ill in isolated places.

Further work

If students are interested in China, divide them into groups of two or three
and give them the following topics to choose from:

— economy   — tourism
— history   — life style
— politics   — geography
— education   — customs

Make sure each group chooses a different topic. They should use reference books and a dictionary, if necessary, to obtain some facts for a short talk about the topic. They should give their talk to the rest of the class.

The passages in units 16, 17 and 18 are loosely connected with travel. You may want to ask students to share their experiences of foreign travel by asking them to write sketches or short essays to display on the wall, bring brochures, photographs, slides and maps to illustrate a short presentation of a recent journey etc.

Unit 19   The capybara

This passage is by Gerald Durrell, who is a well-known naturalist and zoologist. To introduce the topic, you may like to ask if any students keep pets or other animals. Ask them why they have them. Is it for companionship, for food, for protection? Do they think that people treat animals well in their own countries?

You can also ask your students to think of an animal and then, working in pairs, to answer questions about it without revealing its name. The student asking the questions has to guess what animal his/her partner is thinking of. When they have finished one round, they should change roles.

Extracting main ideas

Often it is very important to find a single sentence which sums up the main idea of the passage. You may want to ask your students to do this with future passages in addition to any other *Extracting main ideas* exercises.

Answer:
d) The passage is about the writer's experiences with an unfamiliar animal.

If anyone disagrees with this answer, encourage them to justify their own choice; ambiguous questions will often generate a great deal of genuine discussion!

Inferring

Answers:
a) Because 'the bargaining was protracted.' (line 5)
b) Because they 'gazed at him spellbound' and congratulated themselves on having acquired such a lovely specimen. (line 12)
c) Because they put it in a very strong cage. (lines 7–9)
d) Because it says 'He waited until we were in bed before he started twanging again.' (lines 57–8)

⟫→

e)   Because it says ' . . . or he'll wake everyone.' (line 50)
f)   Because it says ' . . . he's just doing it because he likes it.' (line 48)

Linking ideas

You may want to remind your students that the same idea can often be referred to in a number of different ways.

Answers:
a)   rodent, beast, animal, specimen, creature, culprit
b)   large, coffin-shaped, with a wire-mesh front
c)   curious noise, like someone playing on a jew's harp, someone else beating on a tin can; place his teeth round a strand of wire, pull hard and release it, cage front vibrated like a harp; thumped his feet on the tin tray, noise like stage thunder; harpsichord effect; twanging

Dealing with unfamiliar words

Answers:
1   beheld, gazed, stared, peered, surveyed
2   a) i   b) i   c) ii   d) i   e) i

Understanding writer's style

Answers:
a) iii   b) ii   c) i

Writing summaries

This exercise is designed to show how the passage is organised and how this organisation can be used to write a summary. You may like to turn the headings in 1 into questions, then get your students to answer them without looking back at the passage.

Answers:
1   a) lines 1–7   b) lines 7–13   c) lines 13–15   d) lines 16–20
    e) lines 20–3   f) lines 23–5   g) lines 25–31   h) lines 31–40
    i) lines 40–51   j) lines 50–7   k) lines 57–8

You may like to ask students to read each other's summaries to check if any important information has been left out.

Further work

If possible, try and bring some photographs of wild animals to class. You could organise a discussion on the threats that face wildlife, which will prepare your students for the topic of unit 20.

Unit 20   Save the jungle – save the world

Introduce the topic by asking students to give examples of regions of the world which are being destroyed by urbanisation or turning the land into farmland, or animal species which face extinction. Ask them if they know of any campaigns to save these regions or species. Have they ever heard of the World Wildlife Fund? It is an organisation that is involved in publicising the world's natural resource problems and its aim is to do something about them. You can get more information about the organisation by writing to World Wildlife Fund, 29 Greville Street, London EC1N 8AX, England; perhaps your students might like to write for further details.

Predicting

By discussing the topic before they begin reading, your students will have already begun the process of predicting what the passage may contain. Remind them that there is a lot of information about a passage to be found in the title and the name of the magazine, newspaper, book etc. that the passage comes from. This passage is in fact taken from a brochure produced by the World Wildlife Fund.

Extracting main ideas

Before your students do this exercise, it may be useful to ask them to write a short sentence or two expressing the main idea of the passage. When they have done this, they can discuss their answer with another student. Finally they can do the exercises.

Answers:
1 c) The tropical rain forests of the world are disappearing and the World Wildlife Fund needs money to preserve them.
2 d) The authorities who claim they need the land and its resources.
3 No resettlement of the people, not too much cultivation of the forests, good husbandry, forest ecology, wisdom in planning, less greed and stupidity.

Dealing with unfamiliar words

Point out to your students how certain difficult words and expressions are often explained immediately afterwards or elsewhere in the passage. Encourage them to make a note of the various explanatory devices to be found in this passage and elsewhere.

Answers:
1 a) The tropical rain forest belt stretching around our planet at the Equator.
   b) Man the Builder.
   c) Hunting, trapping, practising a little cultivation.
   d) Forest ecology, wisdom in planning, less greed and stupidity.
2 Commas, dashes, italics.
3 a) alien –   b) pillage –   c) gloomily –   d) monumental +
   e) thrive +   f) meagre –   g) burgeoning +

Linking ideas

Answers:
1) a) Man's   b) the authorities   c) the tropical rain forests
   d) the public, the World wildlife Fund   e) Man
2 a) Because huge tracts of forest have disappeared.
   b) Because the outlook is a pessimistic one.
   c) It is perhaps not the native life style of popular imagination.
   d) If you upset the ecological balance, you have to accept the consequences.
   e) The argument which is destroying the tropical rain forests.
   f) Of the destruction of the forests.
   g) Forests.

Understanding writer's style

Before you do this exercise, it may be useful for students to look through the passage again and decide which words and expressions suggest that it is taken from a brochure rather than perhaps an article.

Answers:
1 He is ironically congratulating the twentieth century for having destroyed so much of the forest.
2 b) In order to emphasise the message.

Further work

You may decide that the preparation for 1 may involve some research in a library. It doesn't matter if the source books are not in English.

Unit 21   Beware the dirty seas

As a way to prepare the students for the topic, ask them to look at the title and to discuss what they think they might find in the passage. Can they think of any examples of dirty seas? What do they think causes this kind of pollution and how can it be stopped?

You can ask your students what town or region is the most polluted in their own country or countries. If they have no pollution, can they think of the reasons why?

Reading for specific information

Answers:
1 Greece, the Israeli Lebanon coast, between Barcelona and Genoa (which includes the Italian Ligurian riviera), the Tyrrhenian Sea, the Po and Venice area, the Rhone, the Ebro, the Llobregat, the Adige, the Tiber, the Nile, and the Bosphorus.

2

Facts about the Mediterranean		*Facts about pollution in the Mediterranean*	
coastal population:	100 million	percentage of world's sea	
number of tourists/year:	100 million	pollution:	50%
ratio of population to		percentage of sewage which is	
tourists:	1:1	untreated:	85%
percentage of world tourist		number of factories polluting:	
trade:	33%	– Ligurian Riviera:	15,000
percentage of world's sea		– Tyrrhenian Sea:	60,000
surface:	1%	– Venice lagoon:	76
number of coastal cities:	120	tons of oil/year from:	
		– ships:	350,000
		– factories:	115,000

Inferring

Possible answers:
Avoid certain parts of the Mediterranean coastline.
Choose a resort where the sewage is pushed a long way offshore.

Avoid eating shellfish unless you know that it is fresh and has been farmed
   in unpolluted waters.
Buy your shellfish from the fishermen rather than in the market.
Avoid the resorts which attract the greatest number of tourists.
Don't swim in the sea.

Writing summaries

If you haven't already done so, ask your students to write a quick two-line
summary of the passage which expresses its main ideas. Then ask them to
check their summaries with another student, and make any necessary
alterations. The emphasis here is not only on accurately expressing the
passage's main ideas, but also on accurate and concise English. You may
find it useful to ask your students not to look back at the passage while
they are doing the first part of this exercise.

Answers:
1 Causes: untreated sewage
            oil and tar
            pesticides and detergents
   Consequences: various diseases
                  danger from bacteria when swimming
                  food poisoning
                  fish killed
                  explosion of plankton
   Other factors: coastal industries
                   high number of tourists
                   landlocked sea, can't clean itself
                   weak coastal currents keep pollution near the shore

Further work

The passages in units 19, 20 and 21 all deal with matters of the environ-
ment and pollution. If the activities in this section do not appeal to your
students, ask them to prepare arguments for and against the proposition
'We need the land for the people; we need the timber; we need the animals
for food'. Get them to present their ideas in a class debate.

Unit 22   The sword that can heal

Ask your students if they know what a laser is, or have ever seen one in use. They are now being used in telecommunications and the entertainment industry, and you can sometimes see them at the checkout counters of large supermarkets, as well as in many other fields. This passage deals with the laser's use in surgery.

Extracting main ideas

Answers:
1 Surgical uses for the laser.
2 paragraph A: e   paragraph B: a   paragraph C: d   paragraph D: b
   paragraph E: c   paragraph F: f

Understanding text organisation

Note that these intruding sentences do *not* belong elsewhere in the passage.

Answers:
'They can even be used to detonate hydrogen bombs.' (lines 4–5)
'This type of cancer is not very easy to reach.' (lines 25–7)
'This technique is particularly useful in ear surgery.' (lines 43–5)
'The beam is diffused to avoid scarring and the mark becomes inconspicuous.' (lines 55–7)
'The beam can cut with a precision that no scalpel can achieve.' (lines 70–2)
'The laser is now being used to treat all kinds of illnesses in this country.' (lines 87–9)

Make sure everyone can explain why these sentences do not belong. Some of them are true but do not make sense in the place where they are printed; others are simply false.

Dealing with unfamiliar words

This passage is taken from a general interest magazine even though the subject matter is fairly technical. Even native speakers of English may sometimes find certain terms unfamiliar and will use the same techniques as those used by your students to look for clues to the meaning.

Possible answers:
b) retina: eye
c) optical fibres: glass, carry the laser beam around corners, direct it precisely
d) enamel: dentist, nerve, hole
e) blood vessels: birthmarks, microscopic, eye, retina

Writing summaries

Before you begin this exercise, it may be useful to ask students to note down as much as they can about the passage without looking back at it. When they are ready, ask them to compare notes and then perhaps write notes under the paragraph headings in *Extracting main ideas* 2. Then ask them to fill in the chart in this section without looking back at the passage but using the notes they have just made.

Answers:

What the laser is used to treat	How it is used	Advantages of using the laser
1 retina	seals individually the blood vessels	only the target is heated
2 cancer	destroys diseased cells	attacks diseased cells, leaves healthy ones unharmed
3 deafness	vapourises the bone	does not touch any of the surrounding tissue
4 birthmarks	seals the blood vessels and conceals the mark	can transform the lives of people doomed to a life of cosmetic concealment
5 peptic ulcers		ulcer treatment without conventional surgery

Further work

This kind of treatment is inevitably fairly expensive. You may like to discuss with your students whether they think that such experimental surgery should be carried out, reducing the availability of more simple operations that many people require.

Unit 23   How to live to be a hundred

In many countries there is a growing number of people who are over the age of 65. Ask your students to discuss the advantages and disadvantages of living a longer life than was usual in previous centuries. Do they think that the best time to retire from work is around 65 or do they think that if people are still healthy, they should be allowed to continue work for as long as they want?

You may also like to ask them if they know of people who have lived a long and healthy life, such as politicians, actors, businessmen etc. What contributed to their longevity?

Understanding text organisation

It is likely that there will be a number of unfamiliar words and expressions in this passage. This exercise, however, is to encourage the students to concentrate on the organisation of the passage. The sentences can be put back into the passage by carefully studying not only their general sense but also the discourse markers.

Answers:
1 1 c   2 f   3 a   4 d   5 b   6 g   7 e

2 a) Some people are naturally more physically active than others.
       but If they take exercise too seriously, it will work against them.
   b) A calm temperament favours longevity.
       but It is important to make a distinction between the calmly relaxed and the passively lazy.
   c) Being successful is a great life stretcher.
       but In gaining success, individuals should not overstretch themselves.
   d) Many long-lived individuals enjoy nicotine and alcohol.
       but In moderation.
   e) Most long-lived people have a sense of discipline.
       but That does not imply a harsh military-style masochism.

Dealing with unfamiliar words

Answers:
2 a) ii   b) vi   c) i   d) v   e) iii

Writing summaries

Suggested answers to 1 and 2:
You should have enthusiasm for some aspect of life. For instance, you should have some kind of hobby.

You should be physically active in a non-intensive way. For example, you should go walking and do gardening.

You should have a calm temperament and a zest for living. For instance, you should take up painting or needlework.

You should be successful in personal terms, such as taking part in local flower shows, or amateur dramatic productions.

You should be moderate in personal habits and have a mixed diet. For example, you shouldn't eat or drink too much.

You should have a sense of discipline and an organised existence. An example of this would be to go for a walk every day, whatever the weather.

You should have a twinkle in your eye, a sense of humour and impishness. For example, you should enjoy the company of other people as much as possible, and be tolerant.

You should live each day to the full. For example, you should pursue any interests you have always promised yourself to take up, and visit the places you have always wanted to see.

Further work

The discussion topics may well cover aspects such as the moral right of doctors to keep people alive by artificial means, the responsibility of the family in looking after their aged relatives etc.

Unit 24　How to help the hard of hearing

This passage is a brochure published by the Health Education Council giving advice to people who can hear on how to help those who can't. Although the passage is about deafness, the discussion after the unit may cover the more general topic of physical disability. One way to introduce this topic is to ask students to work in pairs; one of the students should be blindfolded, while the other should direct the 'blind' person across to the other side of the room without bumping into chairs which have been placed in the way. You may also like to ask them to imagine how the loss of hearing, or indeed any other faculty, would affect them.

Predicting

The title of this passage is fairly self-explanatory. If the students can accurately predict some of the vocabulary and ideas that are likely to occur in the passage, they will understand it better.

Extracting main ideas

It is very useful to be able to decide whether a paragraph has been accurately summarised or not. Ask them to do this exercise in pairs and to discuss the reasons for their answers.

Answers:
1 a) part　b) part　c) complete　d) part　e) complete　f) part　g) part
　 h) complete　i) part　j) part　k) complete
2 a) paragraph D　b) paragraph D　c) paragraph E　d) paragraph E
　 e) paragraph B　f) paragraph C　g) paragraph C　h) paragraph A
　 i) paragraph D　j) paragraph D　k) paragraph F

Linking ideas

a) The sound perceived by the deaf person.
b) When a deaf person has to concentrate on listening.

c) Trying to communicate when the sound is poor.
d) To be absolutely certain of making yourself understood.
e) Useful for helping deaf people.

Inferring

Answers:
a) It sometimes looks stupid or bad-tempered when you stop whatever you're doing.
b) Overlooking things like the fact that you have to speak clearly, slowly etc.
c) Because they will not be able to hear very well and this may make them feel particularly conscious of their handicap.
d) So the deaf person can see the speaker's mouth in order to lipread.

Writing summaries

Before they do this exercise, you may like to ask your students to note as many as possible of the things you should do when you are with a deaf person, without looking back at the passage. When they are ready, they can re-read the passage, and check that they have left nothing out.

Answers:
1 Treat the deaf person as a foreigner.
  Speak clearly, slowly, raise your voice.
  Use pencil and paper.
  Don't obscure your mouth.
  Be sensitive about the surroundings.
  Don't encourage deaf people to go to noisy functions.
  Choose cinemas with good sound systems, and friends who are easier to understand.
  Make sure people are well-lit to help the lipreader.

Further work

Parts of this section may involve the students visiting other parts of the school buildings. You may like to set 2 for homework in order to save time.
   The passages in units 22, 23 and 24 are loosely based on medical matters. It may be a suitable occasion to revise some of the vocabulary to do with parts of the body, medicines and illnesses.

Unit 25   Sorry sir, sorry, sorry

To introduce the topic, bring to class a number of magazine photographs and spread them around the classroom. Ask the students to work in groups of three or four and to choose four or five photographs. They must then try and link the photographs together in a story describing a nightmare journey.

Understanding text organisation

Answers:
1 a) 'Knowing a brick wall when I am speaking to one . . .' (lines 31–8) should go after ' . . . I cannot sell you a ticket from here.' (lines 65–6)
   b) 'I went back to my place at the front of the queue . . .' (lines 47–9) should go after ' . . . claim it back later.' (line 57)
   c) 'When my temper had cooled, I booked a flight out . . .' (lines 82–6) should go after ' . . . nothing I can do about it.' (lines 102–3)

2 a) 5   b) 3   c) 1   d) 6   e) 4   f) 2

Checking comprehension

Ask your students to correct any of the statements which they decide are false. Then ask them to check their answers with another student.

Answers:
a) false   b) true   c) true   d) false   e) false   f) true   g) true   h) false
i) false   j) false

Inferring

Answers:
a) The problem with the writer's ticket occurred when the part representing his flight to London was torn off by mistake. (lines 6–15)

76

b) The writer was not allowed to board the plane without the relevant part of the ticket. (lines 16–18)

c) Even if the ticket with your name on is recorded in the computer, it could still be used by someone else. (lines 39–41)

d) Lines 50–7 suggest that no one had contacted the airline concerned until this point.

e) If you buy a second ticket, you can 'claim it back later.' (line 57)

f) The writer joined the queue for ticket sales with less than an hour before take-off. (lines 31–5)

g) The writer was told at the check-in desk to buy his second ticket from the ticket sales desk. (lines 58–62)

h) The writer says he was told 'We can't deal with new tickets until all the bookings have been dealt with.' (lines 76–9)

i) According to the writer, other airlines have similar rules. (lines 107–9)

Linking ideas

Answers:
a) Eastern Airlines.   b) With the rest of the ticket.   c) You will have to buy another ticket.   d) The name of the person who bought the ticket.
e) About the writer's problem.   f) You will have to buy another ticket.
g) In the queue at the check-in desk.   h) The price of the second ticket.
i) To the check-in desk.   j) On the plane.   k) The whole story of the writer's ticket problems.

Understanding complex sentences

You may like to remind your students that the comma in written English often represents a pause in spoken English, which marks a 'sense group', or phrase which is meaningful in itself.

Answers:
1 a) (i) The supervisor. (ii) He rang Eastern Airlines. (iii) After a long discussion.

   b) (i) In the queue. (ii) We don't know. (iii) We don't know. (iv) Less than an hour before take-off.

Understanding writer's style

Answers:
a) ii   b) i   c) iii   d) ii

Further work

The first exercise in this section would be particularly suitable for
homework. Make sure your students understand that they can invent any
details if necessary.

Unit 26 Go steady on the gas!

This passage is taken from an American magazine, so some of the words are of American English usage. Find out if any of your students have ever been to the United States of America. Do they think that Americans are good drivers? What aspects of driving in the USA did they like or dislike? If no one has ever been to the USA, you can ask the same questions about driving conditions in the students' own country or countries.

Extracting main ideas

Answer:
Get 25% more mpg!
Remember that it doesn't matter if students do not agree with this answer, as some very meaningful discussion will be generated.

Predicting

In fact all these words appear in the passage, although a number of them are rather unexpected. American usage words are: trunk (meaning the boot, or part of the car where you put the luggage), hood (meaning the bonnet, or the bodywork under which lies the engine), gas (meaning petrol).

Dealing with unfamiliar words

Answers:
1 radial tires, tank, windows, air conditioner, engine compartment, snow tires, tire chains, gear, engine, brakes, carburetor
2 a) ii b) i c) ii d) i e) ii f) i
3 a) iv b) viii c) ix d) x e) vii f) i g) ii h) vi i) iii j) v
4 a) tyres   b) carburettor or carburetter

Reading for specific information

A passage like this could easily be read for general interest or it could be read by someone looking for the answer to a specific question. Ask your students to work in pairs and to discuss the answers to the letters in this section. They will only be asked to write suitable replies in the *Further work* section; however, if you've got time and think it a useful exercise, they may like to do this now.

Further work

It may be a suitable occasion to revise some of the vocabulary to do with cars and driving. Think about parts of the car, road signs, types of transport etc.

Unit 27　The Trans-Siberian Express

This passage is taken from a book by Peter Fleming called *One's Company*. The book describes his journey from London to China in 1933 as the foreign correspondent for *The Times* newspaper, and some of the adventures which happened to him while he was there.

Long train journeys are fairly unusual in many parts of the world these days, because most people travel by plane. You may like to ask your students how they would get from their country or countries to some distant place these days. Do people only go by train or plane, or are there buses as well? Can anyone describe how journeys by train used to be fifty or more years ago? Do they think travel was more comfortable or exciting in those days, or do they prefer more modern means of transport?

Predicting

Not surprisingly, the writer was getting a little bored with his stay aboard the Trans-Siberian Express. You may like to ask if your students find long journeys boring as well.

Inferring

The tone of the passage is ironic, so encourage your students to discuss the humour and its intention in these extracts and elsewhere in the passage.

Answers:
a) The vague sense of injustice felt by the author was probably due to the fact that not only was he not expecting the end of the world quite so soon, but he also thought his legs were broken.
b) This suggests that he was annoyed to be woken up so early in the morning.
c) The writer is implying that, so far, everything in Russia had been disorganised and confused, but that the train accident was quite successful as a spectacle.　　　　　　　　　　　　　　　>>>→

81

d) This refers to the incompetence of the staff who were writing different accounts of the event, maybe in order to avoid any blame. The writer is also making fun of Russian bureaucracy.
e) The writer is referring again to the spectacular nature of the train crash, and its probable effect on the child who might expect similar excitement on every train journey.
f) By now he has had enough of his train journey and now it has ended in a surprisingly comic and violent way.

Dealing with unfamiliar words

There are quite a few words or expressions in this passage which are likely to cause some difficulty to certain students. If they have already done a number of the units in this book, they will have learnt that not every word is essential for the general sense of the passage, that many unfamiliar words can be guessed from the context, and that if there are any other words which they don't know, it is better to choose about four or five and look them up in the dictionary than to deal with them all.

Answers:
a) ii   b) i   c) iii   d) ii   e) iii   f) iii   g) ii

Understanding writer's style

Possible answers:
1 'The Trans-Siberian Express sprawled *foolishly* . . . ' (lines 13–14)
  ' . . . which remained, *primly*, on the rails.' (line 19)
  ' . . . the train was dug in, *snorting* . . . ' (line 21)
  ' . . . she had *bullied* us.' (line 44)
  You may also like to point out that most of the last paragraph gives the impression that the train had been a living being, particularly with its use of the personal pronoun 'she'.

2 a) The engine had become detached from the train.
  b) When the whistle blew, we had to leave the platforms in a hurry and get on the train again.
  c) Small boys were always throwing stones at the windows.

3 a) These short sentences suggest that the writer is losing his temper.
  b) Because this luxury train looked ridiculous lying on the embankment and because it was no longer in a position to bully them.

c) Because the other cars were lying scattered around and the word 'primly' suggests not only physically but morally upright, the only car that could remain on the rails.
d) To give an impression of how theatrical and spectacular the whole incident had been.
e) To ironically emphasise the fact that the train was now quite unable to fulfil its original function.

Further work

The passages in units 25, 26 and 27 are all based on the theme of transport. It may be a suitable moment to revise relevant vocabulary using tickets, timetables and other transport documents. Ask students to describe in detail the means of transport used and the documents required for a very long journey. Make a class vocabulary list on the board.

Unit 28   On show

To introduce the topic, ask your students if they ever go to exhibitions of
paintings and sculpture. If so, what was the most interesting exhibition
they have ever been to? Who is their favourite artist? If not, ask them to
explain why.

Understanding text organisation

This exercise type may be a little difficult for some students, but it can
also be a motivating way of showing how a passage is organised. The four
brochures are all written in a similar style, designed to attract the reader
to visit the exhibitions.

Answers:
1   Venice: a h l o   Norman England: b d j k r   National
    Portrait Gallery: c e f n p   Royal Academy: g i m q
2   Venice, Norman England, Paintings from the Royal Academy:
    temporary
    National Portrait Gallery: permanent

Inferring

Answers:
a) No evidence: the passage says that the 1930 exhibition was the last
    great exhibition of Italian masters.
b) True: ' . . . the victory of William the Conqueror in 1066.' (sentence b)
c) True: ' . . . Great or mundane . . . ' (sentence f)
d) No evidence in the passage; it only refers to Venice's Golden Age.
    (sentence h)
e) True: ' . . . will include such great buildings as . . . ' (sentence k)
f) True: 'The Gallery acquires about eighty new portraits a year . . . '
    (sentence p)
g) No evidence; the *National Portrait Gallery* acquires its paintings by
    bequest or gift (sentence p), not the Royal Academy.
h) False: ' . . . and some have never been seen in public before.'
    (sentence o)

84

i) True – Turner: ' . . . Turner (. . .) was still in his twenties when elected'. (sentence q)
    No evidence – Cotman: he is mentioned only in the exhibition on Norman England.
j) True: 'A section of the exhibition will be devoted to the 17th, 18th and 19th century . . . ' (sentence r)

Dealing with unfamiliar words

Answers:
1 paintings, architecture, portrait, sculpture, prints, drawings, ivories, manuscripts, metalwork, stained glass

2 a) ecclesiastical: Canterbury, Durham, Winchester Cathedrals
       secular (buildings not connected with the Church): The Tower of London
    b) positive
    c) large
    d) far apart
    e) portrait; showed
    f) the subject of the painting
    g) a gift

Understanding complex sentences

Answers:
a) (i) the greatest exhibition   (ii) which has been seen
b) (i) the period   (ii) which followed
c) (i) collection   (ii) which has been assembled
d) (i) 200,000 Americans   (ii) who have visited
e) (i) the 17th, 18th and 19th century study of the Romanesque
    (ii) which includes

Writing summaries

The kind of information which is likely to be included in a brochure of this kind and a suggested order would be:
– In recent years, excellent one-man shows of Pre-Raphaelite painters.
– Most comprehensive exhibition ever mounted.
– Vital years of Pre-Raphaelite painting: 1848–60.   ⫸→

– Full range of painting is represented:
   'hard edge' style of Millais' early work,
   seriousness of Rossetti and Burne Jones.
– After 1860, new direction to movement.
– Rossetti: most influential after 1860s.
– Sponsored by Pearson.
– Exhibition at the Tate Gallery.
Other information may be included as well, although the final version
must be similar in style to the passages in the unit.

Further work

If your students have not seen any exhibitions recently, you can ask them
to prepare a similar brochure about a play or a film.

Unit 29 Indiana Jones and the Temple of Doom

The film *Indiana Jones and the Temple of Doom* was directed by Stephen Spielberg, who made films such as *ET* and *Raiders of the Lost Ark*. Ask your students if they have ever seen any films by Stephen Spielberg. Ask them what type of films they like best: thrillers, westerns, romances, detective films?

Predicting

In fact, all of the words in 1 appear in the passage. Some of them, such as *craft* or *cheek*, may be used in a way that is unfamiliar to some students.

Understanding text organisation

Answers:
Sentence a should go after line 61.
Sentence b should go after line 10.
Sentence c should go after line 85.
Sentence d should go after line 116.
Sentence e should go after line 21.
Sentence f should go after line 127.

Dealing with unfamiliar words

Answers:
1 Indiana Jones: improbable −, world-weary −, vigorous +, less wholesome −
  Willie (Kate Capshaw): belly-aching −, comically wry +, giggly ±, blonde?
  Short Round: devoted +, of Eastern origin, Chinese, 12-year-old
  (Note that some of the adjectival expressions used to describe Short Round are neutral in sense.)

2 a) ii b) iii c) iv d) i e) i f) iii g) iii ⟫→

3 a) belly-aching, xenophobia
  b) sidekick, plight, ostensibly
  c) ornate, ram the point home, adversary

Evaluating the text

It may be interesting to ask those students who have seen the film to decide which review they agree with.

Answers:
1 Review 1 thinks the film is bad, review 2 thinks it is good in parts, review 3 thinks it will be successful.

2 a) The style of *Raiders of the Lost Ark* was rather old-fashioned and full of clichés.
  b) Yes, he does like the technique.
  c) No, he doesn't think the director has read a lot of Indian history.

3, 4

	action/suspense	style of film	camerawork/ direction	script
review 1	endless climaxes + 007 stuff +	clichés + originality avoided + pre-war imperial adventure −		
review 2	'cliff hanger' +		camera part of the action +	lack of dynamism − insensitive −
review 3	non-stop action +			little Indian history −

Writing summaries

Obviously, if there are any students who have seen the film, they will be able to add extra details about the plot to their summary, but they should nevertheless try and keep to a limit of about 150 words.

Further work

If your students are coming regularly to your class, it is a very good idea to ask them to write a short review of any film or play they might have seen. You can put these reviews in a place where everyone can see them.

Unit 30   An away win

This passage is taken from a book by Paul Theroux, called *The Old Patagonian Express*.

To introduce the topic, ask your students which sports they like best of all. If they don't like any sports, ask them to explain why not. This passage gives a rather amusing account of a football match in El Salvador, in which the spectators show their support for their team with a great deal of enthusiasm. Ask your students if they can think of any occasions when football fans have become violent in support of their team.

Understanding text organisation

Answers:
paragraph E   paragraph F   paragraph A   paragraph C   paragraph B
paragraph D

Inferring

Answers:
a) Only the Salvadorean spectators are mentioned, and in paragraph E, the stadium was silent when the Mexicans scored a goal, and full of cheers when El Salvador scored.
b) When the ball is kicked out of play, it lands in the Shades or the Suns, so these names refer to the different sections of the stadium. (lines 12–14)
c) '... the slightly better-off Salvadoreans in the Shades section ...' (line 18) suggests that the Shades were more expensive seats.
d) 'The players sat down on the field and did limbering up exercises ...' (lines 23–4) suggests that they did not bother to try and retrieve the ball.
e) 'The Balconies poured water on the Shades ...' (line 16) suggests that the Balconies were above the Shades.
f) ' ... a new ball was thrown in. The spectators cheered but, just as quickly, fell silent. Mexico had scored another goal.' (lines 25–6)

Linking ideas

This exercise is designed to show that sometimes a single idea can be expressed in a number of different ways.

Answers:
Suns, persecutors, Balconies, Shades, Salvadoreans, crowd, Anthill

Writing summaries

As usual, it might be useful for the students to do this exercise as far as possible without looking back at the passage in order to encourage them to use their own words in the summaries.

Answers:
1 a) El Salvador and Mexico.
  b) Mexico.
  c) Fifteen minutes after the match began.
  d) A fight to retrieve the ball broke out.
  e) The players waited patiently.
  f) A new ball was thrown in.
  g) Mexico scored another goal.
  h) Five.
  i) A fight broke out again.
  j) They scored a goal.
  k) The fighting between the spectators.

Further work

If students are interested in the problem of football violence, they may like to discuss ways of controlling it.

The passages in units 28, 29 and 30 are all loosely based on the theme of leisure interests. You may want to revise the vocabulary in this theme by organising a class discussion on 'Leisure in the twenty-first century.' Make a list of the relevant vocabulary on the board.

Unit 31   Should the Press be human?

This passage is written by Katharine Whitehorn, a journalist who has a regular column in the Sunday newspaper, *The Observer*.

The passage is about the responsibilities of news reporters and photographers. Ask your students if they read a newspaper every day, and if so, which one? If not, why not?

Predicting

You may like to ask for a few reactions to the title before you go on to the next exercise.

Extracting main ideas

Ask your students to write down a sentence or two which summarises the main ideas of the passage. When they have finished, they will be better prepared for the rest of this exercise.

Answers:
1 b) 'Should these journalists and photographers join in, or just stand back and watch while people kill one another?' (lines 29–31)
2 d) 'But is there not a point in any profession where you are forced back against the wall as a human being, where a doctor should hand Jack the Ripper over to the police and a lawyer refuse to suppress the bloodstained evidence that proves his client a torturer? I think there is . . . ' (lines 75–81)

Remember that if any students disagree with the answer, you can encourage them to justify their opinions.

Dealing with unfamiliar words

Answers:
1 the Press, photographer, journalist, TV people, sound man, newsman, newshound
2 a) i   b) iii   c) i   d) i   e) ii   f) ii   g) i   h) i   i) i

Understanding text organisation

This exercise should encourage students to be more aware of how the different points of view in an argument are expressed, and how the writer's final conclusion is made clear.

Answers:
1   paragraph A: X   paragraph E: X
    paragraph B: X   paragraph F: Y
    paragraph C: Y   paragraph G: X
    paragraph D: Y   paragraph H: X

2, 3	*argument*	*example*
	lines 17–22, X+Y, 38–53 X+Y, 54–70 Y, 89–99 Y, 100–8 X, 128–31 X	lines 1–16, 23–37, 71–88, 108–27

Writing summaries

Although your students are not obliged to do every exercise in this unit, it is likely that they will find this summary writing exercise much easier if they have done at least *Extracting main ideas* and *Understanding text organisation*.

Further work

You may like to bring a few news photographs into class, and discuss why the editors of the newspaper or magazine chose to publish these particular shots, what they tell us about the subject etc. You may also like to collect together a number of interesting articles with headlines and perhaps pictures. Cut the pictures and headlines from the article and spread them around the room. Ask your students to match the articles with the correct pictures and headlines.

Unit 32   Pregnant Di still wants divorce!

This article comes from the British weekly magazine, *Woman*, and was published shortly before the birth of the Prince and Princess of Wales' second son Henry, in 1984.

Ask your students if there is any subject which the popular press of their own countries is extremely interested in. Do they have any newspapers which concentrate on scandal and gossip rather than on hard news stories? Why do they think this kind of journalism is popular?

Extracting main ideas

Answers:
1 1 d   2 a   3 b   4 g
2 The Princess Di nobody knows (lines 59–63)
   How Queen Elizabeth spends $5.4 million a year . . . (lines 139–47)
   Di fears the curse that's killed five friends (lines 181–200)
3 No, he/she doesn't. Look at the use of inverted commas e.g. in lines 20, 23, 102, 140, 141, and sentences such as lines 26–8, 55–6.
4 'No matter that the "trial" separation was Charles' trip to Africa.'
      (lines 45–6)
   'No matter that this report came five days before her trip to Jordan.'
      (lines 155–6)

Dealing with unfamiliar words

You may like to point out that the register of this passage is particularly informal, which contrasts sharply with the 'formal' subject matter.

Answers:
a) viii   b) iii   c) vi   d) i   e) ix   f) iv   g) ii   h) x   i) vii   j) v

Linking ideas

Answers:
Representatives of the Press: hack, photographers, proprietor of *Truth* newspaper, correspondent, editor of the *Globe*
Palace insider(s): royal observers, close friends, former servant, source close to the Royal Family, Palace source

Inferring

Answers:
a) No evidence; the writer ironically suggests that the stories published about the Royal Family are so varied that there seem to be two separate families. (see lines 1–21)
b) True; see lines 26–8.
c) True; the writer's use of inverted commas suggests this. (see lines 45–6)
d) True; the writer includes the example about the *Sun*'s reporting style to show that she disapproves. (see lines 64–9)
e) No evidence; the writer is only reporting what has been said by other newspapers.
f) No evidence; see (e).
g) True; we can infer he works for the Royal Family because his name is mentioned in the same paragraph as 'The Palace', and this suggests that he is a spokesman. (see lines 117–31)
h) True; see lines 139–47.
i) No evidence; the article says the report came just before the Queen's visit to Jordan, which in effect disproved it.
j) True; the editor of the *Globe* claims that he gets his stories from Palace sources, so they must be authentic. (see lines 202–6)

Evaluating the text

Answers:
a) i   b) i   c) ii   d) iii   e) i   f) ii

Further work

You may find your students attracted by one or the other of the suggestions for *Further work*. 1 will interest students who find this kind of journalism rather unfair and an intrusion on the private lives of people, while 2 will appeal to those who find the whole affair rather amusing.

Unit 33   How do you feel?

You may need to ask your students whether they remember or have heard of the Iranian Embassy siege. It took place in London, in May 1980; opponents of the Iranian government attacked the Embassy and took hostages which they held for six days. The siege was finally brought to an end when the Special Air Service, a regiment in the British Army which is specially trained to deal with this kind of situation, attacked the building. The whole event was particularly well covered by the media. In the passage, BBC refers to the British Broadcasting Corporation and ITN to Independent Television News.

Understanding text organisation

These discourse markers are fairly straightforward, but this exercise may provide a useful opportunity to revise them.

Answers:
1 while 2 when 3 unless 4 when 5 so 6 but 7 while 8 if
9 yet 10 if 11 but 12 if 13 but 14 nor

Extracting main ideas

It might be useful to ask students to write down a one- or two-line summary of the passage in order to help them concentrate on the main ideas. Ask them to check their versions with another student before beginning this exercise.

Answers:
c) The time might have come for the freedom to report certain terrorist acts to be restricted.
d) The present voluntary code of media conduct might, for example, be improved if it could be agreed that the public interest may require certain terrorist acts, involving the seizure of hostages, to be reported only after their release.

Encourage them to discuss their answers as much as possible.

Inferring

The tone of the passage is ironic, so encourage your students to discuss the humour and its intention in these extracts and elsewhere in the passage.

Answers:
a) The writer suggests ironically that the only job they had to do was to eat the meals provided for them. (see lines 11–16)
b) See lines 20–2: 'Unfortunately for the news-gatherers . . . '
c) The writer suggests that there is no reason why the sound technician should have been able to describe his experiences in an interesting way.
d) ' . . . owing to the expectations of infallibility which have been built up . . . ' (lines 65–7)
e) It wouldn't be their fault because 'innocent people can very easily get killed' (lines 76–7), but the SAS are now expected to be infallible.
f) 'To leave terrorists unpublicised would be to render them ineffect-ive . . . ' (lines 84–6)
g) 'There are many freedoms which a civilised country must restrict . . . the classic example being . . . to shout "Fire" in a crowded theatre.' (lines 90–4)
h) ' . . . we can expect London to become a vast TV studio with ambitious performers heading towards it from all over the world.' (lines 110–13)
i) He suggests that they would even be prepared to commit suicide in order to appear on TV. (see lines 117–20)

Understanding complex sentences

Answers:
a) i)   Ate the meals provided for them.
    ii) No.
    iii) To lay down rigid specifications about the provision of meals.
b) i)   Articles about the SAS.
    ii) The ecstatic articles.
c) i)   When fired in confined spaces.
    ii) Yes.
d) i)   By leaving them unpublicised.
    ii) That the freedom of information will not be restricted.
e) i)   It could be agreed not to report certain terrorist acts until they were over.
    ii) Those involving the seizure of hostages.

Writing summaries

As usual, it is a good idea to ask your students to do this exercise without looking back at the passage, so that they can use their own words.

Possible answers:
a) Media gave extensive coverage of siege – but not much going on until the end of siege which happened inside building.
b) Publicity is half the point for terrorists – media gives them stature.
c) Terrorists might invite camera crews inside – rescue attempt might not come off.
d) Because of the fact that freedom of information is not restricted.
e) The freedom to report certain terrorist acts.
f) Should only be reported after release of hostages.
g) Everyone will come to London to commit terrorist acts, certain that they will get the publicity.

Further work

The passages in units 31, 32 and 33 are based on the theme of the media. You may want to ask students to revise suitable vocabulary by asking them to think of ten or twelve words which might belong to this theme and then to check their lists with their partners. Make a class vocabulary list on the board.

Unit 34   Childhood: pathways of discovery

This passage is about the education of infants. Ask your students if they went to infant school or if they waited until they were four or five years old. Do they think their education was the right one for them? Is there anything about it which they regret?

Understanding text organisation

Some students may find this exercise rather difficult. You may decide that it would be better to give them paragraphs 1 and 4 in the correct order and to ask them to re-order only paragraphs 2 and 3.

Answers:

'It has been argued . . . '
'The British psychoanalyst . . . '
'Some people have drawn the conclusion . . . '
'But there are also . . . '

'Firstly, anthropologists . . . '
'For example . . . '
'But traditional societies . . . '

'Secondly, common sense . . . '
'But Bowlby's analysis . . . '
'The possibility . . . '
'Statistical studies . . . '
'Thirdly, in the last decade . . . '
'But tests . . . '

'But whatever the long term effects . . . '
'Children under three . . . '
'At the age of three . . . '
'The matter, then . . . '

Extracting main ideas

Answers:
1 d) Going to school.
2 b) There is no negative long-term effect on infants who are sent to school before they are three years old.
   e) Infants under the age of three should not be sent to nursery school.

Dealing with unfamiliar words

Answers:
1 'day care', 'nursery', 'child care'.
   Ask your students if they can think of any other words used to describe pre-school education: kindergarten, infant school.

2 a) argues   b) analyse   c) decide   d) move   e) suggest

3 a) involves: 'entails' (line 3)   e) examined: 'explored' (line 22)
   b) looked after: 'cared for' (line 6) f) common: 'widespread' (line 26)
   c) damage: 'scar' (line 10)   g) all: 'uniformly' (line 31)
   d) bring up: 'rear' (line 18)   h) handle: 'deal with' (line 35)

Evaluating the text

Before you begin this exercise, it might be a good idea to ask students to say whether they agree or disagree with the suggestion that children should not be sent to school under the age of three.

Answers:
a) 1   b) 2   c) 2   d) 2   e) 1   f) 1

Writing summaries

You may like to point out to your students that a plan of a passage like the one shown in the Student's Book can often be useful when writing summaries. This exercise can be done more easily if the students have already done the exercises in *Extracting main ideas* and *Evaluating the text*.

Further work

If you have students from different countries in your class, it may be interesting to compare the different educational systems.

Unit 35   Village voice

The writer of this passage spent a year in a Himalayan village and wrote about his experiences in a weekly article published in *The Guardian*.

Checking comprehension

Answers:
a) iii   b) i   c) i   d) ii   e) i

Inferring

Answers:
1 The government of the village consisted of some kind of council of
     elders.
   The national government was probably fairly concerned with trying to
     develop its education system in rural areas.
   Village life was fairly traditional.
   The women were obliged to obey their husbands.
   There were probably few facilities in the houses.
   Employment was likely to be mainly agricultural work, which would
     be done largely by the women.
   Leela was some kind of teacher.
   Her job in the village was to set up some kind of education system, not
     only for the children but also for their parents.

2 Probably some kind of malicious stories about her.

Dealing with unfamiliar words

Answers:
1 a) ii   b) i   c) iii   d) iii   e) iii   f) iii
2 a) distrustful   b) were grateful for   c) lazing   d) interested
3 a) behave: act   children: offspring   tasks: chores   brave: daring
   b) small piece: sliver   rely on: depend on
   c) accomplishment: achievement   called: summoned

Writing summaries

You may like to use this exercise for oral practice by getting the students to discuss what Leela has to do in groups of two or three. When everyone is ready, ask each group to present their conclusions. Make sure that everyone includes the same points in their summaries, so that when they have all completed their work, they can exchange and compare versions.

Further work

You may like to extend this *Further work* suggestion into a project in which students can find out about a region of the world which would benefit from some form of aid, and present their conclusions to the rest of the class in some kind of oral or written presentation.

Unit 36   Boys are teachers' pets

Ask your students how they felt about their schoolteachers. Did they feel they were well-treated at school? Were there any aspects of school life which they particularly liked or disliked?

Predicting

Encourage the students to discuss their answers to the predicting questions as much as possible.

Dealing with unfamiliar words

Answers:
1 a) ii b) ii c) i d) i e) ii f) i g) ii h) i
2 *Suggested answers:*
   a) They misbehave.
   b) But girls can be ignored more easily.
   c) Girls are much more concerned with appearances than boys.
   d) The teacher changed his/her opinion.
   e) Teachers favour boys rather than girls.

Writing summaries

Answers:
1 a) Research has shown that boys demand and receive more attention and are better rewarded than girls.
2 a) Girls should be segregated from boys for certain subjects, for example maths and science.

As usual, encourage your students to work in pairs for the exercises in this section.

Further work

The passages in units 34, 35 and 36 are based on the theme of education. Revise the vocabulary in this theme by asking students to talk about their schooldays. Make a list of relevant vocabulary on the board.

Unit 37   Good taste, bad taste

This passage deals with the subject of taste. You should encourage your students to give their own opinions of what they think good and bad taste is, and remind them that there is no right or wrong point of view. The passage was chosen because it seems to be deliberately provocative by claiming to be a factual statement of what good and bad taste is.

There may be one or two references which the students find hard to understand.

Jones(es): This is a very common name in England and especially Wales, and is meant to refer to the typical Briton.

Victoria's reign: Queen Victoria reigned from 1837 to 1901 and her name is often used to refer to a rather strict and moral way of life.

Laura Ashley: A British dress designer well-known for her clothes which were modelled on a rustic style of flowery prints and pastel colours.

Constable: An English painter of the nineteenth century.

Heineken: A brand of Dutch beer which uses some very attractive posters as advertisements.

Cheddar: The most common type of English cheese.

Inferring

Answers:

	good taste	no taste
onyx ashtray		x
Rococo	x	
classical	x	
Gothic	x	
streamlined	x	
Laura Ashley	x	
gold wristwatch		x
Constable reproduction		x
Heineken poster	x	
'Honesty' pattern toaster		x
Cheddar cheese	x	

Dealing with unfamiliar words

Answers:

1 a) dupe −
   b) cynical manipulators −
   c) flashy −
   d) slick −
   e) gifted +

   f) cynical junk −
   g) dignified +
   h) understated elegance +
   i) meretricious ornament −
   j) social pretentiousness −

2 a) i   b) i   c) ii   d) i   e) i   f) i   g) i   h) ii   i) ii

Understanding writer's style

Suggested answers:

a) . . . as the people you're imitating.
b) . . . you might as well inform everyone that . . .
c) . . . I have been seduced and manipulated . . .
d) . . . who have made money out of buying and selling antique furniture.
e) . . . and think about what your possessions say about you.

Further work

There isn't enough room in the Student's Book to include a large number of illustrations, but you may like to bring some magazine photographs to class. Ask your students to work in pairs. Give each pair a selection of pictures and ask them to decide if the writer of the passage would find them tasteful or not. Do they agree with the writer's opinions and his definition of taste?

Unit 38 Shot at dawn

This passage is the story behind a fashion assignment. It is written by the fashion editor of a magazine and describes the arrangements and events of a five-day stay in Egypt to take photographs of clothes in exotic surroundings.

Introduce the topic by asking students if they like fashionable clothes and whether they feel it necessary to keep up with the latest fashions. About how much do they spend on clothes every year?

An additional warm-up activity would be to ask them to close their eyes, or stand back to back with another student, then ask them simply to describe what the other person is wearing. When both partners have finished their descriptions they may open their eyes and turn round and check whether they were right or not.

Understanding text organisation

Answer:
paragraphs A, F, C, B, E, D, G

Checking comprehension

Answers:
a) To take fashion photographs.
b) Five.
c) She was the fashion editor and organiser of the trip.
d) There was no one to meet them.
e) A hotel on the banks of the Nile.
f) Because the light is best early in the day.
g) The hotel staff was fascinated by them.
h) Because their behaviour was so peculiar.
i) She was wearing beautiful clothes and dirty white sneakers.
j) The fashion team.
k) None.

Dealing with unfamiliar words

Answers:
1 silks, satins, jeans, slippers, denim, dress, evening gown, sneakers, high heels, swimsuit, evening gloves.
2 long legs, a cloak of sophistication, resplendent, her mouth painted a brilliant crimson and her eyes shadowed with dusky violet, undoubted beauty and curling blond hair, pretty.

Understanding writer's style

This passage is particularly rich in its choice of words. Some of these will have been dealt with in the unfamiliar words section. Others may be better appreciated by studying them from the point of view of the writer's style. If there are any words or expressions which are still causing some difficulty, you may want to give the students some extra time either trying to guess their meaning from the context or looking up five or six of them in the dictionary.

Answers:
2 a) At the moment she was wearing jeans but would soon be transformed into an elegant princess.
   b) She was able to assume an attitude of sophistication very easily.
   c) I was the fashion editor and the person designated to organise everything and to look after everyone.
   d) The whole photographic session with its dreamlike quality was rather hard to believe.

3 a) treasures: accessories   e) tranquilly: peacefully
   b) dusky: dark   f) poised: ready
   c) peeked: could be seen   g) babble: noise
   d) clutched: held

Evaluating the text

As this is quite a long passage, it may be better for students to concentrate on just one or two paragraphs for this exercise.

Further work

This may be a suitable occasion to revise the vocabulary used in describing clothes and physical appearance.

Unit 39 Absolute musts

The passages and illustrations in this unit are deliberately humorous, so do encourage your students to *enjoy* reading them and doing the exercises. The items are all parodies of articles you can buy in the small advertisement sections of newspapers. It is probably better for students to start to read the passage before discussing their reactions to the topic.

Understanding text organisation

Answers:

2 Cap for two: 6   Woofer: 5   Solarmuffs: 3   Pet-a-vision: 4
   Garbage shoot: 1   Dance instruction shoes: 2

3 Solarmuffs: a i k   Garbage shoot: e n p s
   Cap for two: b d f   Woofer: g l q
   Dance instruction shoes: c j o u   Pet-a-vision: h m r t
   Note: k could also apply to the 'cap for two'.

4 Earmuffs   cap   garbage shoot

Reacting to the text

Ask the students if they find the illustrations and descriptions amusing or not. This is a good opportunity to clear up any problems of comprehension.

Understanding writer's style

Answers:
1 a) You can talk to your partner even when it's noisy.
   b) A long awaited radio.
   c) This artificial pet.
   d) You can wear it with most hats.
   e) You can put it in your pocket.
   f) ... without restricting your arms or legs.

⟫→

109

2 A unit which was not pre-aimed to shoot the projectile into the municipal garbage dump could be used to fire your rubbish at people you don't like, for example.
   a) Obviously the hat encourages the wearers to be very close to each other. The 'complex commitment' might be marriage.
   b) This refers to the fact that animals make your home dirty.
   c) Rover is a common name for a dog; if he wears the 'Woofer' he will be paying you back for the money and effort you spend on him.
   d) Animals often get restless when they are hungry; this device tries to be as realistic as possible by including this feature in its programme.
   e) You can have whatever animals you like, even exotic ones.
   f) 'Taps' refer to the metal pieces on shoes used for tap dancing. Tap dancing in shoes like this may be extremely difficult and for advanced students only.

Checking comprehension

Answers:
a) Small advertisements.
b) In newspapers.
c) Superlative.
d) They make your life better.
e) It is created simply by marketing the product.
f) They are illustrated by photographs.
g) They think they are wonderful and immediately want to buy one.

Further work

The passages in units 37, 38 and 39 are all based on the theme of fashion and design. You may like to lead a class discussion on the importance of design for the successful marketing of new products.

Unit 40   Trials and errors

To introduce this passage, ask students if they can describe how the legal system in their country or countries works. Who appoints the judges? Who runs the legal system? How are juries chosen? What sort of training does a lawyer have to have?

There may be a few questions which they will not be able to answer. The passage may remind them of certain features of their own systems, so you may like to carry on the discussion after they have read the passage.

Predicting

1 This exercise is designed to help the students prepare themselves for what they might expect to find in the passage and to pre-teach a few items of vocabulary which may be unfamiliar.

Answers:
Words that appear in the passage:
lawyer, evidence, witness, criminal trial, prosecution, defence

Extracting main ideas

You may want to ask your students to write a one- or two-line summary of the differences between the British and other legal systems before they begin this exercise.

Answer:
d)   The passage compares the legal systems of a number of countries and discusses their advantages and disadvantages.

Inferring

Answers:
1 a)   True; the writer says it is 'more like a game than a serious attempt to do justice'. (lines 5–8)   ⟫→

b) No evidence; however, the writer does say that 'the object of find-ing out the truth is *almost* forgotten.' (lines 13–14)

c) True; we can infer from the lines ' . . . the Continental "inquisi-torial" system, under which the judge plays a more important role' (lines 22–5) that under the 'adversarial system', the lawyers play a more important role than the judge.

d) Partly true; this happened in England, but not on the Continent of Europe. (lines 34–41)

e) True; in Britain, because the jury couldn't read, all evidence had to be put to them orally (see lines 41–4).

f) No evidence; but the 'exhaustive pre-trial investigation is said to lessen the risk of sending an innocent person for trial.' (lines 54–7)

g) No evidence; however, the passage says that '*much* of it is just a public checking of the written records . . . ' (lines 59–61)

h) True; this can be inferred from ' . . . because the USA has virtually no contempt of court laws to prevent pre-trial publicity in news-papers . . . ' (lines 71–7) and from the fact that the two systems are said to be different (see lines 68–70).

i) True; see lines 75–7 and 'In Britain . . . jurors who are *presumed* not to be prejudiced . . . ' (lines 78–82)

j) No evidence; the passage says that British barristers are kept distant from the preparation of the case. (lines 99–100)

k) True; they are said to 'visit the scene, track down and interview witnesses, and familiarise themselves personally with the back-ground' (lines 89–92). In addition, British lawyers are said to 'approach cases more *dispassionately*.' (lines 104–5)

l) No evidence; all the passage says is that it is difficult to introduce reform bit by bit (see lines 114–15).

2 Britain and the USA: judges do not play a leading role.
France: lawyers play a less important role than in Britain and the USA.

Dealing with unfamiliar words

Answers:
1 a) The prosecution and the defence.
  b) The judge.
  c) Questioning the jurors about their beliefs.
  d) A solicitor prepares the case for the barrister on behalf of the client.
  e) Pleads the case in court to the judge and jury.

2 a) involved: engrossed
       unable to read or write: illiterate
   b) thorough: exhaustive
       included: enshrined
   c) get to know: familiarise
       without taking sides: dispassionately

3 a) to go in different directions
   b) orally rather than in writing
   c) every aspect of it
   d) bit by bit

Writing summaries

Answers:

1

	Britain	*USA*	*France*
'adversarial' system	like two adversaries, the lawyers argue the case in front of a judge and jury		
'inquisitorial' system			judge plays an important role in judging and prosecution
written evidence in court			under the supervision of an investigating judge – pre-trial investigation
oral evidence in court	all evidence given orally		
contempt of court laws	no pre-trial publicity, no questioning of juror's beliefs	do not exist	
random selection of juries	obligatory; presumed to be unprejudiced	not allowed	
role of barrister/ solicitor/lawyer	solicitor prepares case; barrister pleads it	personal involvement of lawyer in preparing case	

2 a) The writer questions whether the British trial system is efficient because the lawyers are more concerned with winning the case than finding out the truth.
3 b) The writer concludes by saying that justice systems could only be improved if they were totally reformed.

Further work

It may be that your discussions have already covered most of the points that would be raised in 1. 2 could be performed as a sketch in front of the rest of the class.

Unit 41   Arresting scenes in Bombay

This passage is about the policing of Bombay in India. To introduce the topic, ask your students if they think there is a great deal of crime in their home towns. If so, what kind of crime is it? It may be useful to revise or teach some of the vocabulary for criminal activities; ask them if they can describe or define the following words:

murder/homicide   manslaughter   robbery with violence   rape
mugging   possession of stolen property   prostitution   assault

You may also like to ask them which of these crimes are less serious than others.

Reading for specific information

Answers:
Bombay: eight million people, over a thousand migrants arrive each day; cramped city on an island.
Types of crime: drug pushing, theft, prostitution, street trading without a licence, entertaining without a licence, corruption. The passage also mentions an instance of abduction, rioting, wrongful restraint, wrongful confinement.

Dealing with unfamiliar words

The clues in this exercise are to help your students work out the meaning of some of the unfamiliar vocabulary for themselves. Encourage them to discuss their answers in pairs.

Understanding writer's style

Answers:
a) Because Manhattan also has a crime problem. The passage is about the policing of Bombay.
b) Conditions in the villages are worse than in the city, or so they believe.

115

c) The front line of troops in a battle.
d) Perhaps because it has a gloomy, unpleasant atmosphere.
e) 'Loom' suggests the area is dark and the figures are vaguely menacing.
f) Because he is someone who may be old and infirm and has lost his human dignity; he doesn't fit into society.
g) That his behaviour was vicious.
h) The interrogation was quite aggressive.
i) No he doesn't.
j) Because, in the conditions of Bombay, it is almost forgivable to commit such minor offences.
k) Because they are only a tiny aspect of the crime problem there.

Evaluating the text

This section gives the students the opportunity to look at both the content and the intention of the passage. If you have time, ask for each group's answers to these questions in a class discussion.

Further work

If the students have already discussed the topic during the introduction to the passage and the various exercises in the unit, they will be fairly well prepared for the group work in 1. If not, you may have to allow a little more time for them to discuss their opinions on the relative importance of the crimes and how to deal with them.

Unit 42 Streetwise

Ask your students if they have ever been the victims of an assault. If so, did it take place in their home town? Are such assaults regular occurrences? What precautions should you take to avoid this kind of crime?

Predicting

This is a very useful way of getting students to predict what is likely to be said in the passage. If there is time, you might like to ask them to prepare a brief sketch in groups of three or four.

Extracting main ideas

Answer:
1 d) The writer relates in a calm way what happened when he was mugged on a hot summer's evening.

Inferring

Answers:
a) True; see lines 9–12.
b) No evidence; he was taking an old friend out, and his wife happened to be away, but there is no suggestion that the two facts were linked.
c) True; he describes himself as feeling 'both philanthropic and mean.' (lines 28–9)
d) True; he replied to the man that he could not give him any money. (line 57)
e) True; he writes ' . . . all this more quickly than I could think . . . ' (lines 65–6)
f) No evidence; he may not have noticed them clearly, but he uses the past perfect tense, as if he had noticed them out of the corner of his eye. See lines 75–6.
g) True; he says 'at least I wasn't kicked for luck.' (lines 105–6)   ⟫⟶

117

h) False; he thought that most muggings are done by coloured people. See lines 118–23.
i) No evidence; the police weren't able to help much, but they did what they could by driving him around the area to identify the attackers. (lines 113–18)
j) True; see lines 117–18.
k) No evidence; the man in the Underground was in favour of the bill. See lines 132–5.

Checking comprehension

Answers:
a) iii   b) iii   c) i   d) i   e) iii

Writing summaries

The exercises leading to the summary writing in this section are less directive or controlled than usual because if your students have already done a number of summaries from this book, they should be becoming more competent and confident about their abilities. However, if this is not the case, you may like to prepare some straightforward questions about the passages which will direct their attention to the most important points, or draw a diagram of the passages to show how they are organised.

Further work

The passages in units 40, 41 and 42 are based on the theme of law and order. Revise the vocabulary in this theme by asking students to discuss the laws they would introduce if they were elected to govern their countries. Make a class vocabulary list on the board.

Unit 43 When a sense of nationhood goes off the rails . . .

This passage is about racism and the treatment of immigrants in Britain. The majority of immigrants in Britain are either West Indians or Asians, usually from India or Pakistan. Ask your students if there is any racism in their own countries. Are there large numbers of immigrants? If so, where do they come from, and why did they choose this particular country?

At the time of writing (1985), Roy Hattersley still has a weekly column in *The Guardian* on Saturdays. If your students enjoy this article, they may like to read some more.

Inferring

Answers:
a) That he had heard this opening sentence many times before and knew that this man *was* in fact a racist.
b) Such an introduction is not uncommon; the writer feels that racism is also very common.
c) The Asians.
d) To help the British and immigrants live more harmoniously together and to keep a check on racial injustice.
e) Because he wanted them to behave like the British.
f) Because to go native implies that the host nation is less civilised than the British.
g) It implies that these are the regulations and treatment that Indians face when they come to Britain. He doesn't 'want to see it' so it is unacceptable.

Understanding writer's style

Answers:
a) A fellow passenger started telling me about himself.
b) When I hear strong opinions, I usually accept them politely.
c) But being polite encourages him to make even more prejudiced statements.
d) I stop being polite.

⋙→

e) The variation last week was something which the speaker really believed to be true.
f) He thought the Asians should abandon the dress and behaviour of their own culture.

Writing summaries

As in unit 42, the summary writing exercise is less controlled, as it is to be assumed that students will have had a certain amount of practice in organising their summaries if they have done a number of the activities elsewhere in this book. However, if you need to help them some more, ask them to write a series of questions about the passage which focus on its main points; then, working in pairs, they should ask and answer these questions, making notes as they go. If possible, they should try and turn their most important questions into the framework for their summaries. Once they have written their versions, they should re-read the passage and check that they have left nothing out, and then compare their work with their partners.

Reacting to the text

This section is at the end of this unit in case the topic is of sufficient interest to be discussed further. However, it may be that all the points have already been dealt with, in which case you will probably choose to pass on to some other activity, such as *Further work*.

Further work

1 would be suitable for project work if you have time.

Unit 44   Lucy Rowan's mother

This passage is about the welfare of old people in New York. The circumstances that Linda Blandford, the writer, describes are not confined to New York, but they often occur in Britain and other European countries. Ask your students if they have any elderly relatives. If so, do the relatives live on their own? Are these the usual living arrangements for old people in their country or countries?

Extracting main ideas

Answers:
1 Lucy Rowan's mother lived alone in Brooklyn – until a few weeks ago, she could still get about – arthritis became worse – talk of putting her into nursing home – Lucy Rowan noticed advert for Early Alert – she telephoned and was told that her mother was not getting all she should be from social security – she called the Department for the Ageing – told her mother would have to wait several weeks before being seen by welfare worker – Lucy moved her mother into her apartment – Lucy discovered that she would have to contact seven different agencies – her mother died before she could work her way through the red tape.

2 Nursing homes, Early Alert, help and money for household chores and personal welfare, various centres and projects, Senior Citizens' Crime Prevention and Assistance Centre.
    Early Alert isn't successful because old people don't like letting it be known that they are old and vulnerable, particularly because mail boxes are often broken into.
    The nursing homes are not at all popular. (We don't know why.)
    Bureaucracy stops people from obtaining all the welfare they are entitled to.
    The Crime Prevention Centre is situated in a rough street off Broadway and there is no elevator attendant.

Inferring

Answers:
a) Probably a welfare worker from the church.
b) It suggests that not many people want to go into the city's nursing homes.
c) The number of the flat in the advert.
d) Because the person had not been down to collect the mail.
e) If the mail boxes were broken into, the criminal would notice the red dot in the box and realise that the box belonged to an old person.
f) Because they might get mugged in the lift if there was no one to accompany them.

Understanding writer's style

Answers:
a) *and* or *but*   b) *so* or *but* (because it wasn't the help that Lucy really needed)   c) *and so*   d) *because*   e) *but*

Further work

2 would be particularly suitable for some project work, if you have time.

Unit 45   Looking on the bright side

To introduce this passage, which is about reporting good and bad news, collect a few newspaper articles that deal mostly with bad news and ask your students to discuss how they would re-write them in such a way as to bring out the good news in them. They may decide that this cannot be done, a conclusion which will be shared by the writer of this passage.

Checking comprehension

Answers:
a) true   b) true   c) false   d) true   e) false   f) false   g) true   h) false
i) true

Understanding writer's style

Answers:
1 a)   Good news and bad news. It will become light.
  b)   Pleasant. The effect of the spectacles is to see the world in an optimistic way. You would only see good news.
  c)   Life is unpleasant.
  d)   No.

2 See lines 00–0.

Extracting main ideas

Answers:
1   Lines 24–33, 45–9, 54–6.
3   First reason f; second reason b.

Writing summaries

The summary writing exercise gives no advice on how to write a summary; if you think that your students still require some guidance, ask them to look back at the writing summaries sections in the earlier part of this book.

Further work

You may have done some of the preparation for 1 if you did the activity which introduces this unit (see page 124). The passages in units 43, 44 and 45 all deal with moral and social issues. The range of vocabulary in this theme can be quite extensive. You may want to concentrate your vocabulary revision on one or two aspects such as the Welfare State, racism, sexism or politics. Organise a class discussion on any issue which may be particularly topical at the moment and make a class vocabulary list on the board.